More Raves

"Wood, as a middleweight, hit his opponents on the head with punches; now he hits the reader in the brain with words. *A Clenched Fist* is an exciting, insightful and inspiring book about the courageous men and women who step into the ring to prove themselves."
—Bert Sugar, internationally acclaimed boxing writer
and former editor/publisher of *The Ring*

"If Peter Wood were as good a boxer then as he is a writer now, we'd be watching his old championship fights on ESPN Classic. He throws a sweet sentence and can knock you out with a paragraph!"
—Robert Lipsyte, author of *The Contender*
and award-winning sportswriter for *The New York Times*

"*A Clenched Fist* is a powerful and painful book. I loved it."
—Kenneth Atchity, president of Atchity Entertainment International

To Alex Ramos — a wonderful Spirit!

A
CLENCHED
FIST

The Making of a Golden Gloves Champion

Peter Weston Wood

Ringside Books

Peter Weston Wood

For further information, please contact:
www.RingsideBooks.com
www.TheSweetScience.com

Front cover painted by Sue Wood

Printed in the United States

A Clenched Fist
1. Title 2. Author 3. Memoir

Library of Congress Control Number: 2006934392
ISBN 10: 0-9789683-0-1
ISBN 13: 978-0-9789683-0-1

Dominic Sgro & Freddie Brown & Dom Bufano & Dan Bufano & George Potterton & Phil Nestele & Philip Freund & Manard Stovall & Sid Martin & Paul Noonan & Kid Sharkey & Charlie Caserta & Father Schroth & Sully Mott & Bobby Lewis

This book is dedicated to

all of The Coaches

who have yelled,

cursed, punished,

praised, guided,

and believed in me.

TABLE OF CONTENTS

ROUND 1

THE PRELIMINARIES

ROUND 2
A RESIGNATION LETTER

ROUND 3
THE MAIN EVENT

EPILOGUE
WHERE ARE THEY NOW?

APPENDIX
THE THIRTY GREATEST NYC GOLDEN GLOVES CHAMPIONS

AUTHOR'S NOTE

This book covers my first year coaching the bizarre underbelly of amateur boxing. Sure, it's a lousy, warped sport. Only lost, twisted souls, like myself, ever step into a ring.

Although some names have been changed, it's all real.

ROUND 1

The Preliminaries

The wildest colts make the best horses.

—Plutarch

I look at my fighter's flat-nosed face as he walks down the aisle towards the ring. He's trained twelve years for this very moment—winning a New York City Golden Gloves title. He swivels his thick neck and throws a few punches in the smoky air. This is his dream come true. *Madison Square Garden.* A dozen years devoted to three rounds. Will he pull it off? Or will he mess up, like so many other times in his miserable life?

I smell victory. I taste it. My stomach's fluttering and my testicles are shriveling, just like the old days. A cold trickle of sweat slides down my face. My kid's sweating, too. I glimpse into his red eyes. I see fear. And hope.

The New York Golden Gloves: a dream, a poem, a stink, a thudding noise, a quality of strength, a pit, a moan, a light. It's a zoological competition where crazy kids punch each other's faces.

The crowd of 6,000 is still buzzing with euphoria over the previous slugfest. ESPN's Gil Clancy, bathed in camera lights, interviews the winner—a Puerto Rican welterweight; his Golden Gloves necklace flashes proudly in the bright lights.

"You can do it," I implore, watching sweat drip from my fighter's chin. I want him to win so bad my teeth ache.

But can he?

The kid's a damn head case. He can easily balance his face, but he can't, yet, balance his brain. Tonight, he's fighting on national television. America is watching. Can he handle the pressure? This isn't one of his crazy street brawls. It's the Golden Gloves. It's when a fighter with a fragile mind cracks.

"Good luck, kid," says Mike Tyson, patting my boy's back at ringside. Donald Trump, standing beside Lennox Lewis and Norman Mailer, looks at us, points, and nods.

"C'mon," I say, prying open the red ring ropes with my back and left foot.

He steps in.

"Loosen up!" I shout above the crowd.

I watch him shadowbox. Kid's beautiful. Better than I ever was. He's mastered every three-punch combination; he slips the hook and counters with incredible speed. His left hook is brutal. He's done every little obsessive thing I've asked—but only when, and if, *he* wanted.

I've clipped his fingernails to make his hands faster. I've cut his hair short so it won't fly when he gets punched. I've given him two t-shirts to make him appear bigger. No chewing gum or toothpicks; chewing saps energy. No sex. No jerking off. There were a lot of small things—feinting at telephone poles and training in blistering heat. I had him do every tiny, petite, infinitesimal thing to get an edge. I was going to do whatever compulsive thing it took to turn this punk into a winner. Just because *I* blew it in the finals seventeen years ago doesn't mean *he* has to.

"Kick ass," I say, stripping off his gold satin robe.

He nods impassively.

He's standing in a puddle of bright floodlights, stripped naked, except for his gold trunks, gold gloves and black boxing shoes. Crowd's hollering and clapping for its hardcore action. I look at his handsome dark face and wonder what he's thinking.

"Seconds out!"

I towel off the sweat streaming down his biceps and cheeks. Kid's sweating bad.

"Feint and throw your right," I whisper into his ear.

I look into his eyes. His *eyeballs* are sweating. No...he's crying. The crazy sonofabitch is *crying*!

The bell rings....

1

A Budding Mike Tyson

*I got lucky and discovered boxing
and some good people who believed in me.*

—*Mike Tyson on how he escaped from the ghetto*

Monday, December 8:

I enter the gym for the first time in seventeen years. I drop my dufflebag to the concrete floor and walk to the ring. "Hello," I whisper.

"Hello," It whispers back.

I look at the blood drops staining the 20-by-20 canvas and I see stupidity.

I feel miserable. I haven't felt this depressed since I was a crazy eighteen-year-old middleweight. But there it all is: the ring, two heavybags and a speedbag that hangs like a black testicle. I grin at myself in the cracked mirror. *What am I doing back here?*

I know the *real* answer, but keep it buried.

I'm the new boxing coach. I start coaching in two days and I already know the kids—fools, lost souls, loners and losers.

Boxing is stupid.

I hate boxing. I hated boxing the day I laced up my first pair of brown Everlast gloves at eight years old. I hated it 14 years later when I quit. But boxing saved my life. Boxing was the blood-sucking leech that fed upon my anger, my hurt, my hate, and my fear. Boxing purified me. That's why I love it.

In two days I'll be introducing this *sport* to a new generation of angry, hurt and hateful boys. What's wrong with me?

Boxing is insane.

Old boxing equipment is stuffed in a gray, punch-drunk filing cabinet. A cloud of houseflies is buzzing overhead. I begin sorting the instruments of torture: brown Ben-Lee, horsehair gloves; cracked Spartan headgear missing straps; rusty Reyes jump ropes without handles; used mouthpieces and blood-stained tee-shirts…

Tami Mauriello sparred with these cracked horsehair gloves preparing for Joe Louis in 1946; Chuck "The Bayonne Bleeder" Wepner, boxed with the brown Everlasts preparing for Muhammad Ali in 1975, and Carl "The Truth" Williams used the black Spartans preparing for Mike Tyson in 1989. I can't toss this junk away—blood and injuries make them sacred.

When I was growing up in Closter, New Jersey, boxing was the only thing that gave me relief. It was the one place where I could drain my anger: onto my opponent's face. Funny, it took me years to discover I had no real talent, but by that time I couldn't give it up because I'd gotten too good. I was a sick puppy, but boxing made me, relatively, sane. It made my blood pump.

As a kid, boxing symbolized manhood, the *key* to masculinity. No more. "Boxing," a fellow high school English teacher chirped, "is the stench in God's nostrils." I laughed to avoid an argument. But there was something he didn't quite understand: boxing is insane yet magical.

Swabbing out the dark filth and dormant rot living inside a glove,

I hear a tiny silent voice within me...*Big mistake. Boxing hurts even those it helps. Boxing's a cure worse than the disease.*
I look into the darkness of Wepner's glove. Boxing is the key to *nothing.* Boxing is yesterday's war. Why go back?
Boxing *is* the stench in God's nostrils.
My mother would agree. She's a beauty queen. She thinks boxing's for barbarians—certainly not her middleclass son who was always punching a heavybag down in the basement below her tastefully-appointed bedroom with peach-colored Austrian draperies and French satin bed sheets. Sometimes I think this etiquette goddess, for all these years, has been my main opponent. I'm not sure why. Maybe because of my arrogant stepfather. But that's another story.

My name is *Irish* Pete Wood. I'm a chubby thirty-five-year-old ex-fighter wearing Gap relaxed-fit jeans. I'm a high school English teacher in White Plains, New York and my blood crawls through my veins like sludge.
I miss running six-minute miles and catching flies in mid-air. I miss the purr within my muscles and the many nights when I found simple spiritual strength pounding an Everlast heavy bag in the basement below my mother's bedroom. I miss boxing.
Last week, this middle-aged black guy sees me shadow boxing on the high school track. We got talking.
"You boxed, huh?" he said. "What a coincidence! I'm looking to hire a boxing coach!" He offers me a job on the spot—$20,000!
So now I'm coaching at Cage, a boxing program funded by Oasis, a national drug abuse program. Cage is an independent branch of The Youth Bureau, a White Plains city agency that offers enrichment programs, AIDS awareness, teen pregnancy discussion groups and adult supervision. It's all an attempt to halt at-risk teenagers' slide into delinquency. It's a noble attempt to keep these little wretches out of jail and out and the morgue. I'll coach Monday through Friday, four hours a day after I teach high school English to sophomores and seniors. The problem is, even I know it won't do anybody any damn good.

But it's twenty grand.

White Plains: the county seat of affluent Westchester County—a miniature Manhattan with a suburban flavor. Donald Trump's new luxury, twin-tower high-rise condos are priced from $950,000 to $4 million. But White Plains is also low-income housing, group homes and halfway houses. In some ways it's the armpit of the area. The White Plains Public Schools, and now my boxing gym, attempt to level the playing field and give the disadvantaged half of the community what it needs—a chance.

While swabbing out Mauriello's old glove, I sniff something putrid. There *is* a stench. I stick my hand inside and feel a furry lump. I pull out, by its tail…a dead rat.

I'll be helping kids, helping kids, helping kids.

Wednesday, December 10:

My first day. Twelve scruffy street creatures sign up. The gym's an old brick warehouse with shattered windows, rusting pipes and hissing radiators. Inside, the air is so hot and sweaty you need to breath it twice to get any oxygen. Pasted on the red brick walls are Joe Louis, Rocky Marciano, Sugar Ray Robinson, Carl "The Truth" Williams and old, faded fight posters. Along the back wall is weightlifting equipment: rusty barbells, a universal machine and chin-up bar. In the middle—a ring.

Two twisted kids climb in and start slap boxing, doing their best miketyson. Their caps are twisted backwards and their funky underwear is sticking out. Ghetto chic. Can boxing save these grubby adolescents from drug addiction and criminality? Maybe they'll catch a whiff of self-esteem. Hey, maybe I'll even get to like a few of these herky-jerky kids, even though I'm not planning on it.

Maybe I *will* discover the next Mike Tyson. The recipe is simple: an angry, hateful, fearful thug who wants to eat your ear.

The closest thing to this concoction is a tenth-grader with an F+ grade average—a boy I'll call Tyrone Crooks. Of course, it's ridiculously premature for an absurd hope like this. But Tyrone is a fighter—at least in the White Plains High School hallways. This Monday he punched a kid through a first-floor window. Miraculously, no one got hurt. Tyrone also mentioned winning a few bouts in Brooklyn, where he was born.

Why does a boy *want* to box? That's the question. Is it because he's a failure in school? Or is it family problems? Is it because he *can't* fight and gets picked on? Is it glory? To prove he's tough? Show me a boxer and I'll show you an unhappy childhood.

I have 12 miserable kids: six Black, four Latino and four White. I divide these mini miketyons into two groups. Sixteen and under are 3:00 to 4:30. I go slow. I ask these Ritalin-soaked guttersnipes to punch each other's out-stretched palms. We play strategy games and agility drills. Each activity is designed for balance and coordination. I praise them. I give them candy. One punk spits on my leather medicine ball when he thinks I'm not watching. Jerk.

The 16-and-above age group is 4:30 to 7:00. We learn fundamentals: stance (with the left foot flat on the floor, toe rotated inward at a 40 degree angle); balance, footwork, and the jab. I keep the atmosphere light. I praise them.

But let's be honest—not a single boy in this gym can write a healthy, comprehensible English sentence. Hell, they probably can't even pass a piss test. No, these are outcasts—shell-shocked boys from non-nuclear families, high-maintenance juveniles with the early earmarking of pathological syndromes. What they need, my beautiful mother would say, is quiet time in a library, reflective time with a child therapist or quality time with attentive parents—not learning how to throw a knockout punch. She might be right.

At 6:00 Tyrone Crooks strolls in eating a packet of Domino sugar. A wild, scuzzy look floats within his eyes. Tyrone's a loud-mouthed syndromeur sporting the young felon look: twisted cap, braids, droopy jeans and designer sneakers. He has *fuck you* written all over him.

"I'm here, man," he pronounces, popping a toothpick into his mouth.

"I ain't your 'man'," I point out, catching the belligerence in his voice. "And take out the toothpick."

He throws three quick punches just short of my head. "I wanna fight *you*." he whispers.

"Anytime," I grin. I look at his wise-ass face—it's a handsome face with high cheekbones and broad flat nose. His little ears are the tiniest ears I've ever seen. But girls love him. He's a charmer, when he wants.

"You gonna drive us to other gyms to fight?" he spits.

Tyrone's the kind of kid I always feared and envied. As a boy I always admired gutsy kids who said *fuck you* to authority. But now, I'm the authority.

He points to the muscular punk standing beside him wearing a silky black do-rag. "Carlos, be my posse. We workout together."

I nod.

Tyrone begins swatting the air. "I hate flies."

"Can't get rid of them," I say.

"Want me to catch you one?" he asks. He points to a fly buzzing around my head. "Betcha I nail him."

"Do it," I say.

"Said I *bet* ya."

I slap down a buck.

"Watch. You ain't gonna believe your fuckin' eyes." Tyrone's eyes narrow into slits. He extends his muscular arm and waits. Suddenly, his right arm whips out. "Got ya!" On his palm is a squished fly.

"I be fast, huh?"

Kid's quick. But I don't like his cockiness. "Bet you can't do it again," I say, slapping down another buck.

"Like takin' candy from a baby," he scoffs.

Carlos chuckles.

"This time I'll use my *left*!" Tyrone's eyes, small and beady, scope the gym. An animal hunter. His top lip curls. He waits…waits…his left arm snakes out. "Got ya!" Grinning, he shows me the fly—black and squished.

"Gimme dollar."

Just then, a pretty black girl jiggles in wearing a see-through blouse with no bra. "Sorry I'm late, Tyrone," she coos.

"Coach, I start trainin' tomorrow." He slings his arm around her shoulder and walks out clutching my two bucks in one hand and cupping her right breast with the other.

Thursday, December 11:

Tyrone never shows.

But others do. A big strong kid with deep-set brown eyes, large nose and 17-inch biceps pops in. I'll call him Kirk Sloboda. Kirk's a landscaper by day and bar bouncer by night. He doesn't impress me as too intelligent. He's monosyllabic. A caveman. We get started on the most important punch—the jab. I show him how to twist his left wrist on impact.

He's got these large gnarled knuckles and he reminds me of a sweaty William Bendix shoveling coal in *The Hairy Ape*. I like the way he works his stiff, awkward body to the bone. What's bringing him to this boxing gym?

At the end of his workout, untying his grass-stained Adidas in the dressing room, Kirk says, "Can I show you something?" He fishes into his dirty dungarees and hands me a piece of yellow-lined paper. It's a poem studded with eraser holes. "I wrote it at work."

"Killer Kirk"
I'm as fast as a bullut going
thru the door.
When I punch you you
want no more.
You will bleed on the
flor.
Of this I am
shure.

"How old are you, Kirk?" I ask.

"Twenty three." He grins.

Thursday, December 18:

Tyrone Crooks and his muscled 18-year-old *posse*, Carlos, strut into my gym sporting tough guy attitudes and intimidating sneers.

"Teach us!" demands Tyrone.

They resemble fighters—or what they perceive fighters to look like. But Crooks' facial confidence isn't a promising sign. Fast or not, he reminds me of a punk willing to work hard, but only if he starts at the top. There's a Buddhist saying: *Before enlightenment, chop wood, draw water; after enlightenment, chop wood, draw water.* Somehow, it applies.

"Okay, Tyrone, show me your stance."

Tyrone plants his feet southpaw and twists his torso righty. It's all wrong. Carlos looks worse; his bony chin is sticking in the air.

But after I correct Tyrone's stance, I discover what I had suspected—he's a natural. I mean, Tyrone's a mean little animal. He can rumble.

Tyrone, grinning, snaps quick jabs at my face. No problem. He reminds me of another walking personality disorder: Steve Taylor, my former high school buddy. Steve died before he was 30. Drowned in puke—malt liquor and hotdog chunks. Maybe if he had found boxing, he'd still be alive.

By the end of their workout, Tyrone and Carlos' sneers melt into genuine boyish excitement.

"When's our next workout?" chimes Tyrone.

"Tomorrow."

"How'd we do today?" he asks, eagerly.

"Okay. What you want, a medal?"

He smiles. "No, *really*, how'd *I* do?"

I don't know if, on the first day, excessive praise is good motivational strategy. But some kids need all the praise they can get. The black/white thing is tricky. The delicate tissue of a black boy's ego, at times, needs a little extra massage. The rough-and-tumble Vince Lombardi approach doesn't cut it here. Brutality and sadism are not viable teaching tools. At least for a white coach with black kids. I'm not editorializing here, I'm just going by the facts as I see them.

"You did good—for the first day," I offer.

"Yeah, thought so, too," smiles Tyrone. Then to hide his enthusiasm, he spits on the floor and walks out.

Five minutes later, someone grabs me from behind. Tyrone. "Gotcha!" he chuckles. "Coach, boxin' be something I can sink my teeth into. I jus' need a chance. And I think I just got lucky."

"How's that?"

"Because I discover someone who believe in me." He hugs me.

Maybe I'm wrong. Maybe this sport *can* reach kids. Maybe I have a Golden Glove champ. A Mike Tyson.

I can't wait for tomorrow!

Friday, December 19:

Tyrone never shows.

But Caveman Kirk does. He's been training with regularity, slowly developing his jab and one-two. He's got a nice right hand, too.

Today Kirk brought two friends—two white high school kids. I'll call them Scrawby Roach and Herbie Pish. Scrawby is a curious creature; a nervous, raw ganglion of a kid with sparkling blue eyes and large yellow teeth.

Herbie Pish is a beetle-browed, vacant-staring sophomore with a thin ferret-like face. Not much talent.

Scrawby juts his dimpled chin towards Herbie. "See him, Coach? I shit on his head last week."

"Did not," says Herbie, softly.

"I didn't pinch a loaf on your head, Mudbrain?"

"No…not *on top,*" clarifies Herbie, looking to the gym floor.

"Coach, Herbie was sleeping on the sofa watching *American Idol* when I squatted over him and pinched a loaf!"

"Are you a pervert, or what?" asks Herbie, softly.

"Why?" scoffs Scrawby. "You lookin' for one?"

"I'm gonna embalm you," counters Herbie.

"And when you do," jabs Scrawby, "I'll have my cremated ashes thrown in your face."

Don't know if Scrawby's pinching-a-loaf story is true, but Herbie seems disturbed. I tell them no trash-talk. In a boxing gym, anger comes out fists, not mouths.

After his shower, Carlos, Tyrone's muscular posse, says, "Coach, I wanna fight bad. *I'm* the next Mike Tyson!"

Wow! A boy's imagination is irrationally rapid; it jumps from knowing nothing to becoming a world champ in two days. "This is only your second day training," I point out.

"Yeah, I know," he says, striking a vicious pose in the floor-length mirror, "but it's *always* been my dream."

"Who you kidding, Carlos? You're 18 and haven't fought a day in your life. So what about your lousy muscles? I think you just want to wear pretty satin boxing trunks, punch people, then sign autographs," I want to say. Instead, I go, "We all have dreams. But you know when a dream comes true? When you wake up."

"Good one. I like that," nods Carlos, toweling off.

I want to support him, but I suspect he's more of a pretender than contender. Tyrone Crooks is who I really want. "Where's Tyrone?" I ask.

"Home. He's doing roadwork at night."

The thought of Tyrone doing roadwork is encouraging. "Why isn't he here today?"

"Dunno," Carlos grins. "But he says he gonna kick your white ass."

When I drive home, there's a letter from my mother. When I hold it to my nose, I smell her cloying perfume. Mom, a beautiful stainless steal tulip, lives in West Palm Beach, Florida. She mails me audiotapes entitled *A Course In Miracles*. Obviously, she still wants to be my shining beacon directing me to higher realms of life. In her opinion, I need help. *"I hope that you've been enjoying my tapes, Sweetie,"* she writes. I'm a former fighter—34-1 with 20 knockouts. How many times have I asked her to stop calling me 'Sweetie'?

The tapes say: *"Your job should spread love. Your business should spread love...."*

Does coaching boxing *spread love?* Tough love, maybe. Boxing *is* a reality-slap that loosens pig-shit inside a boy's brain. Maybe *Sweetie* can reach a criminally prone kid, like Tyrone Crooks.

Why am I wasting time helping a punk like Tyrone? Well, because. The very first day I saw him, he reminded me so much of myself that I broke into a cold sweat. He was slumped in the back row of remedial math class making bathroom noises. He was stewing in silent self-loathing, anger and hate. He was desperate for therapy, but too blind to recognize his need for it.

Last Thursday, I stood in the hallway and peeked into his math class. I gazed at his angry face and began to assume the notion that he *was* me, and therefore, I could become my own teacher and correct myself. Here was someone I knew—a blossoming juvenile delinquent. His little pea brain was shit-loaded. He was someone who might find his natural place, if not *cure*, in the ring. A drastic sickness cries for a drastic solution.

The antagonistic traits—aggressiveness, restlessness, rebelliousness and hostility—that brand a kid as a potential menace to society are also the traits of a brilliant fighter. Crooks is incubating them all. Plus a few. In boxing, craziness *is* genius.

Yeah, there he was, slouched at the desk in the back row of Mr. Benevento's sophomore math class. If you looked at his surly face, he *was* me, or the way, at 17, I imagined myself.

2

Street Mutt

It makes you want to cry to see old friends who failed to beat the trap into which they were born. I could so easily have become one of them. I was running wild and I was either going to end up locked away in prison, or dead.

—Mike Tyson, on his tough childhood in New York, circa 1985

Monday, Janurary 5:

Street Mutt struts into the gym. Some people call Street Mutt a *success* because he's a New York City Golden Gloves 165-pound Champion. But he's also a 23-year old felon recently released from jail for assaulting a cop. The silver ankle bracelet he's wearing isn't jewelry—it's a police electronic monitoring device. There's a lot of ghetto in Street Mutt. He stomps over to a leather heavybag and starts punching.

I turn my mouth in his direction. "Don't hit my bags without permission."

"Shut up!" he snarls.

"Excuse me?"

"Said shut the fuck up!"

"Ask permission," I repeat calmly, "or leave."

"I'll punch you white fuckin' face!"

Nervous sweat trickles through my hair. I set my feet at the 40-degree angle.

He steps closer.

"Leave," I say. "Now!"

He sneers and strides to the door. "I get you—you watch!"

Great. Now I have two black punks wanting to punch my pretty white face. And both could do it. I haven't landed a punch in 17 years.

Tuesday, January 6:

Tyrone Crooks bops into the gym gnawing another packet of refined sugar. I think I'm seeing chinks in his armor. He might not be as tough as I first thought. The Gloves is a year away and I doubt he can train that long. He's probably a loud-mouthed jerk who loses his passion real quick. Well, today at least he's off the streets. Where does he go? Brooklyn? Harlem?

He's warming up in the smudged mirror. Kid's lightning fast. His punches are greased bullets. I've never seen faster hands. I'm in awe. With discipline, he could definitely develop into a Mike Tyson or Kid Chocolate, the great Cuban Featherweight champ of the 1930's, who had to wear white gloves because his punches were so fast they were a blur and judges couldn't count them. Hate to admit it, but Tyrone's faster than I ever was. Hits hard, too. Yeah, he could definitely kick my white ass.

"Tyrone," I say, stepping into the ring. "Let's do fundamentals."

"Fundamentals?"

"First, your head," I say, squaring off with him. "In boxing, it's treated like part of the trunk with no independent action of its own."

"What's a *trunk?*" he spits.

"Your body."

He nods.

"Your chin's pinned to your breast-bone. Got it?"

He tucks his head.

"This position never varies, no matter how your body shifts. If your body turns, your head turns."

"Yeah, yeah, I know all this."

"Yeah, well, listen anyway…Tuck your chin behind your left shoulder…"

"When do I fight?" he goes.

"Later. Just listen," I say, pressing his head down. "Tuck your chin. Good. Now your muscles and bone structure are in the best possible alignment, and only your forehead's open to your opponent." I slap his forehead.

He chuckles.

"See? Doesn't hurt."

"I do it to you, it will."

At the end of the day I'm walking into the locker room—a small cubicle with white flaking walls suffering from psoriasis. Inside are 20 rusty green lockers, a chipped washbasin and a tiny shower stall. Tyrone's sitting on the wooden bench, toweling off his crotch.

"Tyrone, let's talk." I thumb up a green Lifesaver and offer him one. He pops it into his mouth. Crunch.

"Why do you wanna kick my white ass?"

He shrugs, stepping into his jeans.

Such bravado. "Why you cutting school?" I ask.

Silence…Crunching.

"You aren't coming to the gym, either. Why?"

Silence…Crunching.

"I hear you're doing roadwork at night."

"Yeah, so?"

"Tyrone, you know what? You need a good ass-kicking," I want to say. Instead, I smile. "You're capable of greatness—but you need to work," I say.

"You think I'm not working?" he grins, throwing on a shirt.

"Look, you have incredible potential. You're next year's champ. Don't screw up."

"Like Street Mutt?" he says, peeling off the sweaty adhesive tape from his hands.

I nod.

"Wassup wit' chew? He ain't so bad," he says, throwing the tape onto the concrete floor. "He's jus' a brother tryin' to get by in your racist world."

I look at his surly, pouting face. He's played victim so long he's got it down pat.

I fight the urge to slap his face.

"Thanks for the great lecture, Coach. I'll see ya when I see ya." He stomps out with his duffle bag slung over his shoulder.

I pick up the tape he tossed on the floor and toss it in the trash can.

***

Tyrone Crooks isn't my only disturbed prospect. Gym's infested. Take Scrawby Roach, the blue-eyed—yellow-toothed loaf pincher. Today, Malcolm, the gym director, intercepted a *love* letter Scrawby wrote to a freshman girl:

> *Tina,*
>
> *I want your pussy. C'mon, it'll be fun.*
> *My friend Herbie wants to fuck you too.*
> *Yours truly,*
>
> *Scrawby*

For punishment, Malcolm gives him a stern lecture. A real talking to. *Wowie.* For me, Scrawby's doing 500 pushups, 500 sit-ups and 100 pull-ups each day for two weeks.

"She's a sexpot!" justifies Scrawby. "She wears teasy skirts and black fishnet stockings. Maybe it's her low self-esteem. I dig chicks with low self-esteem."

"Your parents teach you to write like that?" I ask.

"Coach, she's a *whore!*" He pulls off his shirt and scratches a rose tattoo on his shoulder. "Last Saturday, three seniors fisted her."

Fisted? I quickly change the topic. "Scrawby, who gave you that tat?" It looks like it was scratched into his flesh with axle grease.

"My dad."

At five o'clock, I discover gym equipment missing: three sets of blue sparring gloves, two striking pads, a pair of red boxing shoes, a dozen rolls of tape and the ring-bell. When I sit down in The Cage office, Malcolm, sitting behind his desk, catches a fit.

"What's it gonna run me?" he spits.

"Eight hundred."

He shakes his head. "Who's the thief?"

Tyrone? Scrawby? Herbie? Carlos? Kirk?

"Let me give you a hint," he says, "keep an eye on a guy named Street Mutt."

"Oh?"

He nods. "Do yourself a *big* favor—keep your eyes peeled."

I nod.

"So" he grins. When can I expect my first Golden Glove champ?"

"Malcolm, I just started." He obviously doesn't understand The Gloves. It's a brutal tournament—a cauldron of anger, youth, and talent. It was started in 1927 by the *Daily News* sports editor, Paul Gallico and has launched the careers of the toughest champions in sports' history: Sugar Ray Robinson, Floyd Patterson, Riddick Bowe and Mike Tyson. New York City is swarming with a yearly batch of young thugs salivating to climb into Madison Square Garden to crack someone's skull.

"A champ looks great for the program," he says.

"Street Mutt was your champ a few years ago."

His eyes widen. "Yeah, that prick doesn't count. He assaulted our last coach. That's why you're here."

"Oh?"

He gets up from his desk and closes the door. "Ugly. Real ugly. At the end of the day, Chuck's taking his usual shower. Thinks he's alone, but someone sneaks up behind him and stabs him good. In the butt. Blood everywhere."

"Someone?"

"Probably Street Mutt."

When I walk to the parking lot, I spot deep scratches carved into the driver's side of my car. Three, long, beautiful jagged scars along the side. All over my hood, too.

Wednesday, January 13:

"They suspended me today," mutters Tyrone, shadowboxing in the mirror.

I sit on the wooden ring stool and listen.

"That teacher with the pony-tail!"

"Rapier?"

"Yeah! He can go fuck himself."

Rapier isn't my favorite, either. He's head of the Honor Society, but thinks he's Lord of the Universe. He's an intimidating social studies dweeb armed with a Harvard degree.

"Screw him! How can he tell me I can't go to the bathroom? He ain't my daddy!"

I hate the weak parts of myself I see popping up in Tyrone. Sad memories sigh within me as I remember my adolescent anger. I recall Steve, my dead high school buddy, lying in puke. We'd skip school and hang out in a Greenwich Village bar guzzling watered-down Schlitz on MacDougal Street. We'd end up on The Bowery staring at bums.

I watch Tyrone paw jabs at the dirty mirror. "C'mon, ya bum!" I yell. "Wake up! Jab twice to the head, twice to the body."

24

Tyrone, not listening, jabs four times to the head.

"Don't you listen? *Twice* to the *head*...and *twice* to the *body.*"

Tyrone still doesn't get it.

I place my hand on his shoulder, and repeat, "Head, *then* body."

"Oh!" he grins. "Why didn't you say so?"

Thursday, January 14:

Caveman Kirk, my other Golden Gloves hopeful, is too slow. Is he suffering from the early stages of rigor mortis? When he jumps rope, his flat plodding feet tangle. But walloping the heavybag, his hands pop!

As I watch sweaty Kirk pound the speedbag, I realize my heart is secretly with Tyrone. C'mon, Tyrone! Wake up!

A coach carries a great responsibility for the development of all his boys. I think I'm beginning to get too tangled up with these weird kids. And now Malcolm's pressuring me for a champion? Maybe I should bail now before I get in too deep.

But I get fired up watching Kirk's bludgeoning right hook, or Tyrone's blistering speed or Scrawby's wicked left hook. That's what keeps me going: the beauty.

Tyrone Crooks never shows. He isn't in school, either. I'm trying to help the little mutant.

Tyrone is high-maintenance. He has no use for education. I suspect his pea brain is telling him: *Why learn a white man's facts and a white man's language in a white man's society?* A guy like Tyrone is going to cause big problems in society if someone doesn't help him.

Teachers and counselors are firing warning shots into his stupid head, but he doesn't get it. Each day, I swear, I feel like jump-starting him with a slap. But, hey, I'm no social worker.

When I get home, I fix myself a cheese sandwich and beer. I'm eating alone in my kitchen realizing something: I, honestly, don't want my life molded by fighting anymore. At age 35, divorced three years, it's time to move on. Somehow, diving back into the sewer of boxing, I'm like a fish who had a long time ago hopped out of the sea to evolve into a higher form, only to splash back in.

Am I listening to my mother's *Course of Miracles* too much?

Friday, January 15:

Tyrone parades into the gym with three gorgeous black girls. New girls. They sit beside the ring, chitchat, and watch him train. Tyrone, stripped to his blue trunks and shoes, flaunts his six-pack. He's certainly a tough-looking stud-muffin. Not an inch of flab.

Kirk Sloboda, my rugged caveman, eyeballs Tyrone punishing the heavybag. There's a whiff of threat and violence in this hot musty gym.

"I hate that kid," mutters Kirk.

Saturday, January 16:

These crazy boxers are getting more and more interesting. Each day at my desk at White Plains High School, after grading quizzes and correcting essays, I jot down notes in a journal. I'm hoping that by writing about my fighters, I'll understand them better.

Since I stopped boxing, it's become my habit to keep a journal. I jab out words and punch out paragraphs. My prose is awkward and crablike, much like my boxing. Writing, like boxing, clears out the debris. It's what they call *cathartic*. My favorite topics: stepfamily, boxing and unconfidence. Since college, I've filled up a dozen notebooks with stepfamily, boxing and unconfidence.

My dad, a professional songwriter, kept a journal, too. When we took walks together he'd jot down random notes and tunes. He called his notes *flyspecks*. Those flyspecks sometimes became beautiful melodies.

Tuesday, January 20:

Herbie Pish is, indeed, a peculiar eighteen-year-old sophomore. Perhaps it's his ferret-like face. Maybe it's his empty black eyes. Or bulging Adam's Apple. Or large oily nose. Yesterday, while shadowboxing, his nose started bleeding for no particular reason. While swabbing out his nostrils, I looked inside his ears and noticed hundreds of blackheads, like poppy seeds, growing inside. Disgusting. Where's his mother?

Herbie also has an annoying habit of smelling his hands. Herbie isn't retarded—perhaps he's dull normal. But something is seriously wrong. It goes deeper than deadpan eyes, poppy seeds and hand smelling.

His life seems to be lived in the dark privacy of his brain. He's always alone, even when he's with Scrawby, his yellow-toothed *friend*. Herbie is fungus-like, soft, yielding and dark. What strange dialogues go back and forth in there? What's life like inside Herbie's head?

Later, Tyrone Crooks strolls into the gym. He hasn't trained in six days.

"Hey! What's up?" I ask, filling a water bottle.

He grabs his crotch. "I knocked *up* a girl, that's wass *up.*"

I look at his angry, confused face.

"What *you* think I should do?" he asks.

"You should come here so I can crack this water bottle over your stupid skull!" I almost say. Instead, I go, "We need professional advice. Let's talk with Malcolm."

"*Sheet*, that old geezer?"

"Isn't there anyone you feel comfortable with?"

"Only you."

My stomach flutters. This kid needs me. "Okay. We'll go see Mr. Mathews, a school guidance counselor. He's cool."

He nods.

"And keep training," I add. "You don't know it yet, but you're a Golden Glove champ."

He grins at the thought, but quips, "I'm still gonna kick your white ass."

Friday, January 23:

It's been three days and Tyrone Crooks, the stupid, ungrateful bastard, finally moseys in for a workout. I don't mention his girl situation. Can't pry.

"Hurry up, Tyrone!" I yell from inside the ring. "We're learning defense!"

Wearing red bag gloves, he slips into the ring. He stands next to Scrawby, Herbie and Kirk.

"Okay, gentlemen—the rockaway. It's a simple counter punch. When your opponent throws his punch, shift your weight quickly to your right leg, and back with the punch. As his punch falls short and folds back to his body, step in with your left jab, and follow with a straight right. Go ahead, practice on each other."

I stand back and watch. Tyrone and Scrawby master it quickly, but Kirk and Herbie struggle. Tyrone is razor sharp. But, unfortunately, he has the personality of a land-mine. People must tiptoe around him. While punching, Tyrone tells Herbie he's going to give him a *dirt nap*. Jerks.

I think as long as Tyrone inflicts anger on inanimate objects, like punching bags, he'll be okay. He's suffering. It's written all over his surly black face. His upper lip curls and he sometimes lets loose with a sharp yelp at the end of a round. He needs to rid himself of his own mental-shit to spare others of it in the future. Tragedy lies dormant in Tyrone like a tumor.

I notice Tyrone and Kirk sneaking angry glances at each other. Problem is, Kirk's too slow and uncoordinated. He'll eat every punch Tyrone throws. Speed can't be taught.

Tuesday, January 27:

My gym is getting popular—a new kid signed up: Bobo Bowe, a squat black 22-year-old welterweight with a 3-2 amateur record. Bobo immediately becomes the gym's alpha dog. He'll spar Kirk and Tyrone when they're ready. He'll demonstrate moves, build their confidence and be their security blanket. It's always safest when there's one experienced fighter in the ring.

Bobo's a stutterer. I like stutterers. I st-st-utter myself. There are too many cocky Muhmmad Alis walking around. Sparring inexperienced kids will also boost Bobo's confidence. It will allow him to practice the scarier maneuvers—right uppercuts, or lead rights to the belly (both punches expose you to your opponent's right hand, usually his best shot) without risking a black eye.

If I had a son, would I let him box? No. He'd hit *books* instead of *people*. Boxing is the worst way to grow a healthy boy. I'm a hypocrite.

Thursday, January 29:

At the end of the day I swing my black, key-damaged Mitsubishi Galant out of the gym parking lot, past the sanitation department and up Kensica Avenue. Strutting down Lake Street is my future Golden Gloves champion. His arm is draped around another cute black girl.

"Yo, Tyrone! Where've you been?"

"Oh, snap!" he says. "Jus' be coming to see you!"

"You in school today?"

"Nah, I just comin' back from the clinic."

"Everything okay?"

"I *eliminated* the problem," he smiles. "Thanks." He then spots the deep gouges ripped into the side of my car. "Wow! Someone got you good!"

"You know who?"

He gently fingers a deep gouge. "Nah, man." But his expression says otherwise.

"You'd tell me if you knew, right?"

"Nah, nah, I ain't got no idea who did nothin'."

A quintuple negative! I'm a high school English teacher and have no clue what he meant. Maybe that's the idea.

"Coach, I'm training tomorrow. I'm your Golden Gloves champ!"

Friday, January 30:

Tyrone never shows.

I'm sitting at my kitchen table writing this journal. I think I'll keep it informal and in first-person. I'll use present tense and add dialogue, if I can remember it. Keep it real.

I'm not going to write everything there is to write about the boys and me. I've read those stories, completely precise and detailed, nothing omitted. They're informative, but it's not my style. I'll *adumbrate.* That's my father's word. It means *to outline in a shadowy way* or *to suggest.* Dad's music was that way: sweet, delicate and ethereal. Maybe that's why I became a boxer—to balance him out. Anyway, that's why Dad disliked Bach. Too many notes. Dad said Bach sounded like a sewing machine.

I'm surprised at my poor spelling and grammar. Actually, I'm not. I was never a grammar genius. And when I write a quote I always forget if the period belongs *inside* or *outside* the quotation marks. I'm a guy who needs to rely a lot on intellectual equipment—dictionary, thesaurus and spell-check. Words like *alot, likeable, athlete and grammar*, they always allude me.

Who keyed my car? Street Mutt?

3

Sculpting Beauty

Me—
Whee!

—Muhammad Ali, an impromptu poem
composed during a college speech

<u>Monday, February 2:</u>
    I'm beginning to like these knuckleheads. Coaching boxing is sculpting beauty into a boy's body and brain. When a boy moves sweetly, that's art. It's chiseling a human statue. Martha Graham sculpted ballerinas; I'm sculpting fighters. She educated toes—I educate fists.
    A boxing gym is a factory where a boy's muscles and self-esteem are forged. Dom Bufano, my trainer, said that. He forged me. But he missed with the self-esteem part. I work so hard to be confident, but even after 35 fights, lack of confidence is still deeply embedded into my flesh. So how can I plant confidence and self-esteem it into these boys, if I don't have it myself
    Can I sculpt Malcolm a Golden Gloves champ? I doubt it.

Tuesday, February 3:

Today, Scrawby and Herbie Pish don't speak much, but that's okay. Dom Bufano once said *Speech isn't important in a boxing gym. I can explain and motivate with a silent vocabulary.* He's right. A pat on Herbie's back, a warm smile or a friendly nod says it all. And Scrawby's fists hitting my punch mitts communicate his emotions better than any eloquent phrase. Spending one grueling hour in the gym, postponing all conversation, is enriching. Aldous Huxley wrote *Speech is an inferior form of silence.* I like that.

I've always distrusted eloquent people. My stepfather and some teachers at White Plains High School are eloquently stupid.

Language doesn't go as deep as feeling. But Herbie's left hook—even his grunt—does. There's no grammar to a grunt. Like higher math, boxing transcends language. A boxer exists on instinct; only his mind trips him up. When I fought, I set myself on "automatic." Mentally, emotionally and verbally I was pretty shabby. You're only as strong as your weakest link—and my weak link was my mind.

Still is.

Now I'm an English teacher. Sometimes, I feel like a fraud. I was profoundly mediocre in all subjects—except gym. Me becoming a high school English teacher is like a criminal returning to the scene of the crime. But I've cleaned up okay. But my mind still lags two steps behind. I still suffer from word-retrieval. In second grade it kicked up. I remember when I wanted to say *door*, but couldn't. In the White Plains High School teacher's lounge, an empty coffee cup out-debates me. Yesterday in class, while teaching *Flowers for Algernon*, I couldn't think of a simple word: *forgiveness.*

I turn to watch clumsy Kirk hit the heavy bag and quip, "You're a mule." It was a compliment, like *You hit like a mule.* Tomorrow I'll clarify myself. I don't want him thinking I consider him to be a slow, stupid-beast, even though I do.

Wednesday, February 4:

Think a boxing gym is violent? Try my classroom in White Plains High School.

Sitting before me are young sharks: upwardly-mobile sophomore workaholics blessed with aggressive minds. They are privileged and programmed to within an inch of their lives. They streak through their fun-filled days: tennis lessons, Bloomies, private tutoring.

Today we're writing the persuasive essay.

"I'm writing about the merits of breast implants," says Isabella.

"How about legalization of marijuana?" asks Matt.

"Cloning," states Fang.

"All excellent topics," I nod.

Zoe, a girl with a t-shirt that reads: *So Many Books, So Little Time*, slowly raises her hand. "My topic is boxing. It should be outlawed."

Matt swivels around in his chair. "Why?"

"It's sadistic, that's why," she says. "Boxing isn't even a sport."

"That's crazy!" Matt erupts. "Ban cigarettes, not something that's been around since Ancient Greece."

"Yes. Boxing is a throwback—to the caveman. America shouldn't sanction assault and battery."

"Boxing's an art," says Matt.

"Muhammad Ali has brain damage," she grins.

"No, Parkinson's Disease," he counters.

"No, he's punch drunk."

It's a boxing match—two fighters, an audience, and I'm the ref.

"Okay," punches Matt, "why not ban bullfighting or football? Or *Nascar?*"

"Maybe we should," Zoe jabs. "They're all violent."

"Should we ban dodge ball?" he scoffs.

"Some schools have!" she counters. "There's no redeeming value to dodge ball. Besides, it hurts self-esteem."

"Hurts self-esteem?" gasps Matt. "So does musical chairs!" Matt looks at the kids in the class. "The real problem isn't violence—the real problem is America's getting soft."

A few students clap.

"Boxing is sick," clubs Zoe. "We have laws prohibiting dog fights and cockfights, so why is pitting two men against each other perfectly legal? We regulate *poultry* better than athletes."

A few students clap.

"Soft microsoft lives? That's advancement?" counters Matt.

"I want less violence," she slugs. "There are healthier *things* than boxing."

"That's my point!" counters Matt, pounding his desk. "The healthiest *things* in life aren't *things*! They're *ideals*—strength, determination, sacrifice, courage. Boxing teaches that!"

The class applauds.

***

Fifth period a loud commotion outside my classroom.

"Fight! Fight!"

I sprint down the hallway.

Shrieking. Yelling. There's nothing like a fistfight to draw a crowd. It's better than Shakespeare.

"Don't look at me in that tone of voice," shouts a voice.

It's Tyrone. He has an upper-classman pinned to a locker by his throat. His balled fist is sticking in the boy's frightened face.

I pry them apart, drag Tyrone into an empty classroom, and close the door. He slams the blackboard with his elbow, spits on the floor, and kicks a desk. His mental illness is really kicking up. After punching his face, he slumps into a chair.

"What happened?" I go.

"Nothing," he spits, kicking another desk. Tyrone goes silent. Then he blurts, "Why don't you hit me, or something?"

"Why? You haven't done anything to me."

"Why you always trying to help me?" he says.

"What's eating you, Tyrone?"

A full minute of silence…Now two.

"...Kid reminds me of my father." He pulls out a cigarette and sticks it in his puss.

"Take it out. You're in school."

"You ain't my daddy," he blurts. He lights it up and inhales.

I reach over, but he smacks my hand. "I'm faster than you," he sneers.

"Get rid of it. Cuts stamina."

He grabs the cigarette from his mouth, kisses it, and stuffs it back in.

"Mike Tyson quit."

"Who the fuck is Tyson?" he scoffs. "I'll be better'n that punk, you watch." He inhales a good lungful. "You ain't gonna turn me in for fightin', are ya?"

I look into his wise-ass face. I wonder.

"You turnin' me in?"

I'm thinking about it, but I get a better idea. "I'll give you a break. This once. If you stop smoking."

He takes a deep pull, mulls it over, throws the butt onto the floor and stomps on it. "Deal." He hands me the Marlboros from his shirt pocket.

I point to the butt on the floor. "Pick it up."

He stoops down, picks it up, and flicks it in the trashcan.

"One more thing," I say. "Remember when you were holding that kid by his throat?"

"Yeah?"

"Your form was bad."

"What?"

"Your right elbow was sticking out too far." I stand up and demonstrate. "It should be here, see? Pinned to your stomach. And your chin, remember? Pin it to your breast-bone."

He chuckles. "You crazy, Coach."

Perhaps I am. Maybe I am enabling bad behavior. Maybe I should report him. But if he's going to be next year's Golden Glove champ, he needs to know these things. Cutting him slack once won't hurt. Just once.

Thursday, February 5:

Tyrone never shows. So much for sculpting beauty.

But Lola, my first girl boxer, signs up. Many coaches don't encourage girls, but I'm okay with it. I welcome females because it's unique. It's not like she's whispering *unsex me here, and fill me, from the crown to the toe, top-full of direst cruelty.* It's simply refreshing to see a gutsy female willing to scrap. If she wants to get her nose broken, let her.

Sing-Sing Tu, a new special education teacher from our high school, walks into the gym. She's a pretty Chinese woman with silky black hair, slim hips and long thin legs. I've noticed her sashaying down the White Plains High School hallways, but I've never said hello. Shouldn't she be modeling? The beauty mark on her top lip is Cindy Crawfordesque.

"I heard about your boxing club at school," she smiles, wiping perspiration from her brow. "Phew! It's hot in here!"

Ninety Five degrees hot.

She smiles as she watches sweat pour off Herbie, Scrawby, Kirk and Lola as they do push-ups, sit-ups, leg raises, neck bridges, hit bags and skip rope.

"I'm sculpting beauty," I say.

"And teach English in room B-122, right?"

I nod.

"Then come here every day?" she smiles.

"Three o'clock till 7:00."

"You're very dedicated."

I shrug. Smile. "You should meet Dom Bufano."

She tilts her head.

"My former coach. Dom's like a priest or guru. He treats kids like flowers." I tell her about how Dom specializes in the quiet, sensitive kids. He understands their psyche. He sees an introspective boy as having the biggest heart because he has more to overcome."

She smiles. "Was he your catcher in the rye?"

I glance away.

"Do you believe your boys are flowers, too?"

I shrug. "Some are weeds."

This philosophic moment is soiled when Scrawby Roach hawks up a clam and gobs on the concrete floor.

She grins.

After watching my flowers, she bends down and kisses Herbie's moist, pink cheek. I notice her black skirt riding up her thighs.

"I see London, I see France…," sings Scrawby. His fat yellow teeth gleam with saliva.

"Focus on your bag!" I bark.

"I am!" he quips. "My scrotum bag."

"Give me 200 push ups!" I bark. I turn to Sing-Sing. "Sorry about that. That boy's a dog."

"Yes, I know. I have him in class."

"And please," I add, "don't kiss my fighters—women ruin legs."

She smiles, walks up to me and plants a kiss on *my* cheek. "Yes. Children *are* flowers," she nods.

4

Jump, Kirk, Jump!

Rocky Marciano stuck out like a rose
On a garbage dump.

—Jimmy Cannon

Kid Corbett, an eighty-five-year-old pro trainer, stops in to take a
look. He's a gray, dungeon-colored man, who—though stooped—is
still, essentially, vertical. He has the face of a well-worn nickel and little tufts of wheat-colored hair, like beards, grow from his cauliflower
ears. I know why he's here.

"You stealing my fighters?" I ask. I'm concerned, primarily, about
him sinking his meat hooks into Tyrone Crooks.

Corbett waves me off, laughing. It's a rough laugh that sounds
like crackers are stuck in his throat. His mouth is full of decayed nine-
teenth century teeth. It's rumored he recently broke a molar sipping
potato soup. But we both know why he's here: he's scouting talent. A
pro trainer fishes muddy water to spot new prospects.

He begins dropping names. "Carl 'The Truth' Williams is back in training. We're lookin' for a crack at the heavyweight title. And did I tell ya' I'm workin' on a Roy Jones-Dave Telesco match-up at Radio City Music Hall?"

Kid Corbett like kid Skarkey another local trainer is a font of boxing information. His life's boxing.

He married his third wife in a boxing ring. How ironic.

Years ago, Kid Corbett informed me about Mike Tyson. "Tyson's gay," he said.

"No way."

"As a three-dollar bill," he chuckled. "How you think his old trainers, Cus D'Amato and Jimmy Jacobs, died? AIDS. Faggots! Where you think Tyson dredges up his rage? He's sex-conflicted. How many women he beat up? Tyson's a sex monster."

Recently, I asked two ex-pros working up at Gleason's Gym in Brooklyn to verify Kid Corbett's story. Both had been former pros under Cus D'Amato in the early 1950s, and both knew Tyson. Both grinned and nodded.

Mike Tyson, gay?

Corbett, with his hands folded into his armpits, watches Kirk train.

Kirk's too slow to master the rockaway, a basic defensive move, so I have him parrying punches instead. It's easier.

Kirk and I square off in the ring. "Okay, Kirk, parry my lead left with your right hand. That's right. The movement is more wrist than arm. You got it. No, don't move your elbow. Catch my jab on your wrist, not your glove. Good! Then lower your left hand, ready to counter my body..."

"His jab looks like he's reaching for a donut," grunts Corbett.

"Yeah," I say, "but his right hand can hospitalize a brick."

"If it lands," he scoffs.

Even though he won't admit it, Corbett is impressed with Kirk's raw power.

"Kirk's my next Rocky Marciano," I boast, toweling him off.

In truth, Kirk's still in the larval stage. After two months, he's only beginning to *resemble* a fighter. He's gracefully clumsy and developing hints of speed.

But when Kirk jumps rope, I'm depressed. He's terribly terrible. His big flat feet get ensnarled in the rope and I ask myself: *Is boxing a healthy form of therapy, a beacon of light, or just an on-going expression of a problem?*

Kid Corbett shakes his head, "Your Rocky Marciano is a knockout waiting to happen."

Maybe. But Corbett is still eyeing Caveman Kirk with interest. If I don't watch it, Kirk will be working out in Corbett's gym across town. The old man's a thief.

Truth is, I suspect that Kirk's not emotionally conflicted enough. Anger is essential, and a healthy dose of abnormality is helpful, too. Unfortunately, Kirk's too emotionally healthy for his own good. He doesn't have enough curvature of the brain.

Mike Tyson once quipped, "Doing what I do and normal don't go together."

Friday, February 6:

I'm dead tired. Six o'clock this morning, before school, I look at my tired face in my bathroom mirror. The fleshy pouches beneath my eyes look like exhausted poultry. I've got too many student essays to grade, too many fighters who will get beat up, two fighters who threaten me, a boss who pressures me, stolen boxing equipment, a keyed car, and a future Golden Glove champ who doesn't train. I'm peopled out.

During a free period, I catnap in the teacher's lounge.

I'm helping kids, I'm helping kids, I'm helping kids...

"Hi!"

My eyes snap open. It's Sing-Sing.

"So, what'll you teach your *flowers* today?" she grins, setting a stack of student papers on the desk beside me.

"Balance," I yawn. "Three-punch combinations. Jab-right cross-left hook..."

She snaps three sharp blows, karate style. "Like that? *Baba* taught me."

"Baba?"

"My daddy. He called me The Little Terror of Mott Street!"

"You from Chinatown?"

She nods. "I'm ABC—American Born Chinese. My parents emigrated from Guangzhou when I was four."

"What got you into teaching?" I ask, sitting up.

"What got *you* into *boxing*?" she asks, turning it around.

"Well, my stepfather was a scumbag, my stepbrother was suicidal, my stepsister was mentally ill, my real brother was a junkie, and my mother, don't get me started on my beautiful mother," I want to say. Instead, I wave her off.

"*O-kay*...What got you into *coaching* boxing?"

"Some guy saw me shadowboxing on a track."

She smiles. "That was *meant* to happen." She leans forward and her jade necklace swings gently against her black silk blouse. "There are no accidents. He was *supposed* to see you." She leans closer. "Peter, do you believe in miracles? I know I'm you don't really know me and shouldn't be spouting off, but students today," she taps her stack of student papers and shakes her head, "need a miracle—a big fat miracle. Teachers can work miracles."

I shrug.

"Maybe even boxing coaches," she grins. "Well, I'm not sure on that one," she adds. "You are, after all, instructing children to hit each other on the head."

I don't want to hand her the line: *Boxing is a sick way of getting healthy*, so I just shrug. Boy, is she pretty.

Wednesday, February 11:

Gym's sweaty hot. Every rusty radiator is belching steam and the red brick walls are perspiring. Sweat's dripping everywhere.

I'm working two blistering rounds on the punch-mitts with Kirk, Bobo, Lola, Scrawby and Herbie. *Then* Tyrone.

After his two rounds, Tyrone becomes child-like.

"I like it when you work with me," he grins, spitting away sweat.

"I like working with you, too. Where've you been?"

He shrugs. Perspiration drips from his chin.

Bell rings.

The next round I slap his forehead repeatedly with stiff jabs. His upper lip curls. He's grunting like a dog as drops of sweat from his hair spray into my face.

At the bell he howls and smiles. "I like it when you hit me."

I find that interesting.

Thursday, February 12:

Kirk Sloboda finally masters the jump rope! *Hooray!*

See Kirk jump! Up and down! Jump, Kirk, jump!

Everyone cheers—except Tyrone.

Tyrone's leaning on the ropes, sneering. "Hey, slowpoke! It's gonna take more'n footwork to beat me!"

"Up yours!" blurts Kirk, throwing down the rope.

They stare at each other with all their might.

I like this.

At the end of their workout, I gather up my boxing team—Caveman Kirk, Stuttering Bobo, yellow-toothed Scrawby, weird Herbie, Lola, and Tyrone. They look like bizarre, sweaty figures from a Hierony-mous Bosch painting.

"We're *brothers*," I say. "We're White, Black, Latino, and remember—we're fighting *with*, not *against*, each other." I raise a hand and spread my fingers. "Each finger is different, but together…," I clinch my fist to make my point, "…we're strong!"

Herbie Pish's dull eyes brighten. "Oh! We're family!"

"Yes, Herbie," I nod. "We're family."

Kirk and Tyrone glare at each other from across the ring.

At 6:00, Kirk calls me over and points to my photo on the wall.

Someone scratched out my eyes and wrote above my head "Dead Meat!"

"Probably Tyrone," he whispers.

Or Street Mutt.

Friday, February 13, 1998:

This morning I walk into my classroom, B-122, and smell something delicious. Sitting on my desk is a Tupperware box. There's a note taped to it:

"FOR A COACH WHO SCULPTS BEAUTY"

The Chinese steamed buns inside are still warm.

5

That Boy's a Diamond in the Rough

I was a schizophrenic when I met him.
I soon found out he was a schizophrenic, too.
The four of us have gotten along fine ever since.

**—Patrick Flannerty, *Macho Camacho's*
former schoolteacher**

<u>Friday, February 13:</u>

"*Dead Meat!*" is still bothering me.

If someone wants to make me *dead meat*, would I stand a chance? Probably not. I haven't fought in years.

The truth is this: After I stopped boxing at 20, my blood never flowed as fast. Drabness set in. It's like my spirit was subtracted out of my flesh. That's why most fighters average two to three comebacks. They ask themselves *Is there life after boxing?* And the answer is *No.*

I hung up the gloves and attended Fordham University. I started hitting books instead of people. I was an ex-middleweight hiding in the back seat of classrooms, nervously chewing the inside of my cheek. After 35 fights, I had to accept the fact that in the classroom arena I was second string. My untrained brain and s-stuttering t-tongue weren't as potent as my fists. Getting verbally bitch-slapped by a witty thinker was always a concern.

One day in the Fordham library, while struggling with Spinoza and wrestling with Rousseau, I arrived at a horrible thought: as a boxer, I was physically tough because I was mentally weak. Was the size of my biceps really the size of my weakness and fear?

***

Kirk, grunting and sweating, thrashes the speedbag—*Thwack! Thwack! Whoosh! Thwack! Thwack! THWACK!* Suddenly, the bag rips off its swivel and smacks onto the brick wall.

I hand him a dollar. "Good job."

I really admire this slow, muscled middleweight. There's quiet strength to him and he's slowly improving. But Golden Gloves champ...?

If Kirk had Tyrone's raw talent and Tyrone had Kirk's work ethic, my boss Malcolm and the city of White Plains would have *two* Golden Gloves champs.

At the end of the day I make a startling discovery in the gym's locker room. Lying on the damp concrete floor is a beautiful, long-legged, naked blonde. Her tongue's sticking out and she's licking the cherry off a vanilla cupcake. She's a *Penthouse* pinup. This is the second soggy pin-up I found this week. Who is leaving them? Maybe it's my new pro middleweight who sometimes comes around...Al "Tiger" Green?

Monday, February 16:

I walk into the locker room and announce: "Everyone be here tomorrow! Someone important is coming!"

"Who?" asks Kirk, whisking off forehead sweat with his thick forefinger.

"Dom Bufano, my former trainer, head coach of Bufano's Gym."

"We sparring?" asks Tyrone.

"Not tomorrow."

"I know eight moves!" Tyrone crows.

"By now, genius, you should know all thirteen," blurts Kirk. There's a clenched fist in his voice.

The *eight moves* Tyrone does know are from Dom Bufano's "13 Moves of Boxing." It was my Boxing Bible. I've laminated it and taped it to the brick wall.

THE 15 MOVES OF BOXING

1. Jab
2. Double Jab
3. "Hook off the Jab"
4. Jab—Right Hand ("One—Two")
5. Left Hook To Body—Right To Head—Jab-Jab
6. Right To Body—Left Hook To Head—Jab-Jab
7. Left Hook To Body—Left Hook To Head—Jab-Jab
8. Right To Body—Right To Head—Jab-Jab
9. Jab—Right To Body—Left Hook To Body—Jab-Jab
10. Jab—Right To Head—Left Hook To Body—Jab-Jab
11. Jab—Right To Head—Left Hook To Head—Jab-Jab
12. Flurry (6 Fast—6 Hard)
13. Parry Jab with your Right—Counter with Jab
14. Parry Right—Counter with Jab
15. Parry Right—Counter with Right

Remember: PAIN IS WEAKNESS LEAVING THE BODY

—Dom Bufano

Tuesday, February 17:

Dom Bufano enters. He's a former lightweight, a feisty game-cock, with a flat, squished nose and cauliflower ears. He sports fuzzy, white hair and a milky eye which, he claims, was thumbed by Tony Canzoneri, a lightweight champ in the 1930s. I put him at 82.

Noise hits Dom first: the loud thud of the heavybag, the smack of the jump rope, the machine gun whap of the speed bag.

Then smell. Zoological odor and spicy sweat waft through the hot unventilated air. Dom looks at the brick walls, then up at the clogged air vents, furry with black dust and oily dirt. He smiles. It's not a clean gym and I caution all of my boys not to go barefoot—especially when showering.

Dom walks into the locker room which is lit by two bare bulbs hanging from the ceiling. He whisks open the shower stall curtain. The filthy stall gives everyone pause. Everyone's secretly concerned about the germs, scabies and ringworms that lurk in there. Everyone tiptoes in hoping for the best. The smart thing to do is wear rubber thongs, but that would admit weakness.

What unnerves me most about the stall—and I keep complaining to Malcolm about it—is the thick, cheese-like sludge on the tile floor. I hate that. I think the brown sludge is what is responsible for the flabby brown odor. People piss in there, too. I'm sure of it. Today I whisked back the flowery shower curtain encrusted with black mildew and caught Scrawby Roach pissing.

Dom appraises the rusty green lockers, the sweaty adhesive tape thrown carelessly in the corner, the chipped porcelain sink and the unwashed handwraps hanging on a nail stuck in the crumbling brick wall.

"I see you don't clean up much," he says.

"Well, I…"

"No, that's good," he interrupts. "Keep it that way." He breathes the stale ugly air, opens the toilet stall with the tip of his shoe and inspects. More flabby brown odor billows out. He nods. "My first gym, back in the 60s, I thought I'd give my boys something special, so I cleaned it spic-'n'-span, painted the walls nice and fresh and that was a big mistake. I had a bitch of a time getting' the boys back. These guy like it the filthier the better."

"Why's that?"

"Makes 'em feel more at home."

Dom's boxing royalty. At least in Jersey City. He's developed count-less Golden Glove champions. In the same way that certain dogs sniff cancer in people, detect earthquakes, or predict epileptic seizures in their owners fifteen seconds before they fall, Dom spots genius in a fighter. He's psychic. That's why I'm blessed he recognized something special in *me*. But it was Dom's gruff gentility and earthiness that first attracted me. He fosters almost a mystical communion with his fight-ers. I remember the day he took me under his wing. I was 12 when he held my shoulders and kissed my forehead. "Hey!" I blurted.

That's when he told me this story…

I grew up in Harlem. My dad deserted me when I was 12. I began box-ing. Kept me outta trouble. One day I'm sparring in Grubb's Gym on 116ᵗʰ Street when Sugar Ray Robinson, my idol, walks in. I wanna impress him so I spar hard. Sugar Ray be so amazed, he said, 'Honky, you good!' Then he kissed my forehead! Robinson said, 'Honky, when I be your age, Joe Louis watch me in the gym and he kiss me on my forehead. Louis said, 'Kid, take good care of that kiss, cuz it come all the way down from the great Heavy-weight Champion, Jack Johnson, who gave it to me! Now I give it to you.'"

I was 12 and my Dad just died. It was a blessing to have Dom in my corner. Dom became my coach, my friend, my father. That day he kissed *me* on my forehead and passed *The Jack Johnson's Kiss* down to *me* was utter magic.

Jack Johnson…Joe Louis…Sugar Ray Robinson…Dom Bufano…me!

Nothing in my life has meant so much as that *Kiss*. Dom's praise was an antidote to my father's death. It was a candle in the dark. It was magic. It was love. He said I was a tough little kid, and that meant the world to me because I knew, deep down, I really wasn't.

With Dom, I went 34-1. With 20 knockouts.

But, fuck me, I lost in the Golden Gloves Finals.

That's why I want Dom to meet Tyrone Crooks.

But the stupid idiot never shows.

At the end of the day, disappointed, I walk into the bathroom and enter the stall. Suddenly, a shadow from behind taps my shoulder. Tyrone!

"I did it again, Coach." His face is puzzled, sad and angry. "These womens're killing me."

"What are you talking about?"

"Got another bitch pregnant," he mutters.

"What exactly happened, Tyrone?"

"Well, me and this girl be raw-doggin' in her room, this bitch from the group-home up the street."

"Talk right, Tyrone! She's a *girl*, not a *bitch*. Is this the same girl you were walking with the other day?"

"Nah, that be another b—girl. Well, we be in Elizabeth's room, door's locked, and I'm, ya know, inside her. And I'm, ya know…" he lifts his stiff forearm and smacks it.

"Hard? Erect?"

"*Really* hard! I'm about to, ya know…"

"Ejaculate?"

"What's that?"

"Come?"

"Yeah, explode!" he grins. "But she hold me inside her tight 'cause she want my baby."

"You piss me off, Tyrone," I say. His energy is going into his cock, not boxing. The boy's governed by groin.

"Help me, Coach!" he hollers, throwing a jab at my face.

"Look, we'll speak with Mr. Mathews again. He'll know how to…"

"Bullshit!" he says, spraying a haymaker in my direction. "Can't let the school know nothin' no more."

"How about your mother?"

He bangs the locker with an uppercut. "No way."

"How about, I don't know, a church minister?"

"I don't do religion," he says, slapping the sink.

Our conversation is degenerating into an incomplete success.

"I'm sorry, Coach. I'm letting you down."

"Look," I say, "tomorrow we'll talk to the school psychologist."

He looks at me sideways. "You think I'm crazy?"

"You're nuts, Tyrone! Absolutely sick. Totally pathetic!" I want to say. "Of course not, Tyrone. We need a new perspective, okay?" He seems relieved.

Then he adds, "Coach, I like how you say *we* when you talk about me and you."

I smile. "Go outside, there's someone here *we* gotta meet."

Dom throws Tyrone a pair of bag gloves. "Hit the heavybag," he orders. Tyrone begins thrashing it with an explosion of ecstasy and craziness.

"This kid's a diamond in the rough," Dom whispers. "Wish I had him. Fuckin' kid's nuts."

"No shit."

"You gotta tap into him."

How? It's easier said than done. I haven't the tools.

Next, we watch Tyrone bob and weave in the cracked mirror. Dom grins and says, "Kid reminds me of you."

Wednesday, February 18:

Sing-Sing stops me in the school hallway between classes. "Tyrone Crooks is failing everything. I mean *everything*. He's hardly attending. We're trying to get him out-placed. Maybe BOCES can train him in automotive maintenance or computer repair. We've tried everything, but we're not meeting his needs."

"Whenever I ask, he says he's doing fine."

"Fine?" she scoffs, "That boy's blind!"

I'm blind, too. Secretly, all I think about is Tyrone Crooks, my Golden Glove Champ, bringing me back to Madison Square Garden. I can't just give up on him. "Boxing can help him," I say.

"That's right, boxing is art therapy."

She's being sarcastic, I know, but she's young, still thinking inside the box. She can't perceive that a kid might, just might, find guidance and direction by using alternative methods.

Then she sighs, and her sigh seems to release steam. "I'll stop by your dirty, little sweat box tomorrow and see how your *art therapy* works."

Today, in period 4, I look at the fresh eager faces in my sophomore English class and see myself…"Hey what do you teenagers secretly think about yourselves? Are you happy? Sad? Do you like yourselves?
I write on the board: "A teenager is…." I want to ask
Some written responses:

A teenager is…
    …rebellious, but if given freedom, she will choose the right read.
    …a human being with strong feelings and weak judgment.
    …obnoxious and annoying.
    …a ketchup zebra.
    …born from the eyeball of Kurt Cobain.
    … a target for cigarette companies.
    …a concept so dynamic that we must be categorized in a slippery ideological group hovering between child and adult. In a nutshell, we are very mature kindergartners or very immature adults.
    … a ticking time-bomb.

Thursday, February 19:
    Tyrone Crooks punches into my gym office and picks up a two-inch End-swell from my desk—(a metal training device which I freeze in an ice bucket, then press onto a fighter's face to reduce swelling.) He's flipping it up and down.
    "Well, you crazy sonofabitch, you're finally here to kick my white ass!" I think.
    "I'm quittin'," he says. "My family's breakin' up. My mom's movin' to South Carolina. She's gettin' re-married. I gotta live with my crazy brother and get a job. I can't box no more."
    His eyes tear up.
    "I don't know what it is, Coach," he says, "I always *wanna* train,

but there be always somethin' stoppin' me…I'm lettin' you down, Coach, and I feel bad."

I feel manipulated and touched at the same time. I think Tyrone *needs* to box. He needs toughness on a deeper level. But is the pull of the streets too intoxicating? Is boxing too demanding? Is he too weak? Is this the end of the road for Crooks? Maybe boxing was never his road in the first place.

Maybe it was only my road.

That night, at suppertime, I call Mrs. Crooks on the telephone. "Hello? This is Coach Wood, Tyrone's boxing coach."

"Yeah, he mention you. What you want?"

"Tyrone said you'll be moving down South."

"He did? Where down South did that damn fool say I be movin'?"

"South Carolina."

"Uh huh."

I hear her exasperation. "If he needs a place to stay, I'll help you locate something."

"That's awful nice, Woods. Yeah, I be movin' south—but only two miles south. I moving' down the road, to Mt. Vernon, two towns south. That ain't no North Carolina. That stupid fool son of mine won't be needin' no room. Unless, of course, you wanna give him one."

"Well, I'm sorry about the misunderstanding. But since you're on the phone, if I can be of any help—tutoring, counseling—here's my phone number."

"Thanks, Woods, but only thing that damn kid be needin' is a good ass whuppin'. Can you do that fer me?"

"Well, I…"

"Nah, didn't think so. I'll beat his stupid black ass myself."

6

A Nervous Twitch

*I was a mediocre amateur
who developed into a competent professional.
But I'm really just a never-could-be.*

*—Bruce "The Mouse" Strauss, Omaha
middleweight with a record of 76-52-5*

<u>Friday, March 6:</u>
"Damn, Wood, it's sweltering in here!" complains Malcolm, wiping the pops of sweat from his forehead. He looks around. "So, who's my Golden Gloves champ?"

"They're *all* champs," I state.

Malcolm flashes me a weak grin as he watches me slam a leather medicine ball into Kirk's iron gut.

"Where's our...OOF!...sparring gloves?" grunts Kirk. "Can't be your...OOF!... Golden Gloves champ if I don't spar."

"Keep your shirt on—they're coming." Then Malcolm turns to me. "Coach Wood, you crank it up too hot in here. You'll kill them."

It's 95 degrees. Dom Bufano kept his gym at 95.

"Get...OOF!...my gloves!" grunts Kirk. "I'm your next...OOF!...champ!"

"No, I am," shouts Scraby. "No, m-m-me," stutters Bobo, throwing a left hook through the hot air.

Monday, March 9:

Where's Tyrone? He probably discovered what most kids discover: the fantasy of being a fighter is much better than actually being one. The euphoria wears off quick. Let's face it, boxing isn't ever, really, fun. It's scary. You don't bring boxing gloves to a picnic. Boxing is fighting disguised as sport; anger disguised as play. "Punching people is a hell of a way to make friends," said George Chuvalo, a former heavyweight contender. But Indira Gandhi said it best: "You can't shake hands with a clenched fist."

Let's face it, I'm not sculpting beauty. I'm teaching a squalid, antisocial activity. When you watch Mike Tyson perform, you watch an ill man display sickness.

Tonight, turning off the light in the locker room, I find another sex kitten hiding in the locker room. She's lying in the shower stall—a beautiful brunette from *Hustler* playing with the thick end of a pool cue. Who's doing this?

Tuesday, March 10:

I'm noticing a nervous twitch developing in the masonry of Kirk Sloboda's face. And I suspect there's damp fear hiding beneath his armpits. Is it because he knows he'll be sparring soon? It's said, *The English kill their lamb twice; once when they slaughter it and once when they cook it.* A similar thing is beginning to happen to Kirk: he's getting beat up twice, once in his mind coming to the gym and again when he's in the gym.

Kirk's stumbling toward mediocrity.

Where's Tyrone Crooks, my Golden Glove champion?

The bullshit of hope.

7

Denial Is The Essence Of Boxing

The first Joe Frazier fight in Jamaica was the most scared I've ever been in my life. I didn't want Joe to look down because if he had looked to the floor, he would have seen my knees shakin'.

—George Foreman, former Heavyweight Champion

Wednesday, March 11:

Tonight three sets of blue, 16-ounce, Ringside sparring gloves arrive. I smell the cool leather and slip my hands inside. They're superior ergonomically—more comfortable and lighter than my old Everlasts. I crouch into my boxing stance in front of the mirror and see myself at 18. I throw a few punches. How would I do with Stuttering Bobo? Tyrone? Kirk?

It's no fun being an aging athlete. I drop down and do 30 push-ups. All the time, I see Sing-Sing's beautiful face, black silky hair and long thin legs. And my soft paunch.

Thursday, March 12:

Stuttering Bobo and Kirk are standing in the ring, greased, ready to spar.

"Box nice—no wars," I whisper into Bobo's ear. "You need to spar him again."

"Box nice—no wars," I whisper into Kirk's ear. "You need to spar him again."

Kirk is yawning with nervousness.

I hope all of Kirk's hard work and dedication won't amount to scar tissue and brain damage.

Waiting for the bell, they swivel their necks and eye each other. When I boxed, this was when the back of my testicles shriveled up— I hated that.

Clang.

Kirk lunges forward and hammers Bobo first. Kirk is as scientific as a mallet. Bobo isn't as speedy, or cagey, as I had hoped—he's getting caught with too many punches. It's like watching two inexperienced hurricanes in the same paper bag.

After two rounds of messy mayhem, Kirk wearily stumbles through the ring ropes. His red potato face looks parboiled. "Give me two more rounds," he gasps.

"Save it for tomorrow," I say, wiping his sweaty face in his soiled blue towel. "Good job today."

Bobo, still fresh, boxes two with Tiger Green, the pro middleweight who came in a few weeks ago.

Where's Tyrone Crooks?

Friday, March 13:

A boxing gym isn't a room; it's a *state of mind*. There's always free-floating hostility flying around. I watch these young kids work out and wonder what strange silent irrational thoughts squirm through their young minds. Well, when I left the gym last night, some joker proved his toughness by sticking a metal thumbtack in my light-bag.

This afternoon it's as flat as a pancake. The jerk probably wanted to stick that thumbtack up my ass, or jam it in his father's butt. Who was it? Tyrone? Scrawby? Herbie?

Also last night, some malcontent kicked an eight-inch hole in the wall. Last week I walked into the gym and found the mirror shattered. *Nah, nah, no one knows nothin'.*

And there was another sexy wench hiding in the locker room last night—a voluptuous blonde in black fishnet stockings and stiletto heels.

Who is doing this?

Monday, March 16:

At the end of his workout, Kirk walks into my office. He's chewing the flesh on the inside of his cheek. He sits down. "Coach, what can I do about...you know..." His rugged face looks emotionally fragile and I know the precise word he's avoiding: *fear.*

"The nervousness?" *Nervousness* for boxers is our euphemism for *fear.*

He nods.

"Kirk, the more I think about boxing, the stupider it seems. It's ageless stupidity. It goes smack against everything Western Civilization stands for. But, maybe, just maybe, in this hot, grungy boxing gym, I teach one extremely rare, valuable and crucial human value."

"What?"

"It's found under your left nipple: *courage.* Without courage there would *be* no Western Civilization."

He's still chewing the flesh inside his cheek.

I love this caveman and I want to comfort him. I tell him what Dom Bufano once told me: "Kirk, no one *conquers* fear. Boxing teaches *resistance* to fear, *mastery* of fear. But you never lick fear."

He looks at me and asks a pretty good question. "When you were fighting, how did *you* deal with it?"

"I ignored it. I gulped it down." I wish I was smarter, but it's the only answer I know. Boxing's about tricking yourself into believing in yourself. Denial is the essence of boxing.

I look at Kirk gnawing his cheek. I want to pump him up with reassurance and hope. "Kirk, boxing's good, I suppose, because you're *passionate* about *something*—even if it is bashing in a guy's face. At least you ain't curled up in bed watching Spongebob."

When I leave for the day, I walk to my car and find a brick has smashed through my windshield. Shattered glass everywhere. I pick up the brick from my front seat and find a message attached. It reads:

DIE WHITE YUPPIE SCUM!

I call the White Plains Police and file a report. They say they'll keep their eyes open.

8

Hey, Coach, What Got you Interested in Boxin'?

My cause is me.

—Joe Frazier, when asked why he didn't have any causes, as Muhammad Ali did

Tuesday, March 17:

"Hey, Coach," says Caveman Kirk, swiveling his neck, as I helped him put on his favorite ringside bag gloves. "I was just sort of wondering—what got you interested in boxing?"

How do I answer Kirk honestly? Do I say: Kirk, I was one pissed-off, thumb-sucking, bed-wetting, stuttering, asthmatic, butter-hearted pussy until I converted from Christianity and Judaism to Boxing. Do I explain how I read *The Diary of A Young Girl* and identified with Anne Frank? My stepfamily were my Nazis. Do I tell Kirk that I suffered through it, smiled through it, because, pussy me, found it too scary to stand up to my stepfather? Do I explain how I identified with Blacks? Not that I envisioned myself chained to a slave ship eating slop from a dirty wooden bucket in between whippings, but my family was also decimated.

Should I explain the plumes of pollution in my pre-adolescent brain? The anger running through my veins? The ten miserable years of boxing rings and leather boxing gloves? Do I explain how my beautiful blissed-out mother living in utter denial contaminated us with a dysfunctional stepfamily? How she sold us out for the country-club life, the maids and status? How she had us living well above the poverty line but a million miles below the emotional line?

Should I rehash my stepbrother's suicide attempt? My stepfather's alcoholism? My brother's heroin overdose?

My mother's denial. Her immunity to reality. Her smile. She's worst of all.

Thanks, Mom.

Should I tell Kirk that I've always hated boxing but seemed to have derived a weird masochistic pleasure from it? Would Kirk be interested to know that I still chain myself to things that I can't do? Like writing.

Should I get philosophical: Boxing was like falling in love—I did it for selfish and irrational reasons; it was self-motivated—yet I did it and discovered it was a good idea?

Should I tell him that when I trained in Dom Bufano's crazy gym I never felt I was in the right place, but, like a mole clawing into a small home under the earth, that dark, lonely place was the *only* place?

Should I tell him I screwed up in the finals?

Should I tell him to get the hell out of this stupid, fucking boxing gym before it's too late?

"What got me into boxing?" I shrug, pulling on his glove. "Fighters were always my role-models: Golden Glovers, prelim kids and main-event fighters on *Friday Night at the Fights*. Later, the tough kids in school were my heroes."

"Then you became one, right?"

"I *tried*." This is all very true, but I was never really a fighter— by genetics, anyway.

"I can tell you were a tough sonofabitch," he smiles, jabbing my shoulder. "You know a lot."

He doesn't need to know how lame I really am. He doesn't need to know that inside his rough tough boxing coach are soft pillows and wall-to-wall carpeting.

"So, Kirk, what got *you* interested in boxing?" I ask, turning it around.

He frowns, tapping his gloves together. "Coach, it sucks being told your whole life you're stupid when you know you aren't. So, I come to the gym between jobs. A lot of my friends go home to sleep or eat pizza, but I come to learn."

"Learn?"

"You see, Coach," he says taking off his right glove, "I could do alotta other things with my time. Learn trumpet. Take a landscaping course…" He rubs a crumb of dried blood from his nostril, examines it, and flicks it to the floor. "Yeah, my nose hurts, but so what? Gotta spar to get good, right? My girl, Mitzi, thinks I'm nuts. But I can't be champ if I don't spar. I've been training five months. I did the math: an hour and a half a day is 45 hours a month." He throws a few lazy punches. "Coach, in January, a good friend of mine died. Motorcycle accident. Billy looked up to me. Always said I was one tough sonofabitch. When I'm bouncing at night, or cutting grass I think of Billy. Don't get me wrong, I like landscape, but I don't wanna be buried in wet grass. Boxing is, like, my outlet to express myself, to let Billy, and White Plains know I ain't just a working-class stiff." He nods and smiles. "I'm tough as nails, Coach."

"Yes, you are." I place my hand on his shoulder and tilt his head. "Nose hurts?" Gently, I finger the bridge then wiggle it. I look up his nostrils checkting for a break. Looks okay. I ruffle his sweaty hair and hand him a box of Q-tips. "Clean your nose—it's the only one you got."

The blessing of a bleeding nose.

The Talmud sums up the Jewish perspective on child-rearing in one sentence: "A father is obligated to teach his son how to swim."

Jewish wisdom holds that children don't belong to us. They are both a loan and a gift from God, and this gift has strings attached. Our job is to raise our children to leave us—to give them strength and confidence.

Boxing is like swimming—isn't it?

9

I Have Disturbing News

*I like girls. White. Black. Purple-striped.
It's all the same to me.*

**—Ken Norton, NABF
Heavyweight Champion, 1973**

Wednesday, March 18:
    The hot gym is thick with steam and the air above the corroded radiators is wiggling.
    Clang!
    Kirk Sloboda scuttles from his corner and starts punching. Sweat flies from his headgear. His sweat-soaked T-shirt reads: **I'M NOT TOO SMART, BUT I CAN LIFT VERY HEAVY OBJECTS.** Watching Kirk spar Bobo Bowe is like watching a monkey paint with a paintbrush. Despite his determination and training, Kirk's not *really* improving. Perhaps there's a profound purposelessness to what we're all doing here.
    I'm not Kirk's father and boxing isn't swimming.

"Jab and move," I say, wearily. "Move your head!" It's not that Kirk isn't tough—in a back alley, he'd cripple you for life—but in the ring he's dead meat. Nothing's sinking in.

Clang!

Kirk's charging forward like G.I. Joe, his flat feet are plodding the canvas and Bobo is bayoneting his face with sharp jabs.

Kirk swivels his reddening face towards me. "I SUCK!" he bellows.

"*Move!*" I implore. He isn't doing *that* badly; he does manage to get in a few hefty wallops.

But after eating a right hand, Kirk snaps. He starts flailing his hairy arms. He's going ape-shit. Konrad Lorenz, the great social scientist, once wrote: *Few lapses of self-control are punished as immediately and severely as loss of temper during a boxing bout.*

In my opinion, no good boxing gym can operate without a kid getting a black eye or a broken nose every once in a while. No matter how careful you are, or how many precautions you take, it's going to happen. I don't like to see my kids get battle-scarred, or have their egos squished, but this is boxing. It's not pretty, sometimes. If they don't like it, there's always Aikido or Tae kwon do.

Thursday, March 19:

Period 3, I spot Tyrone loitering alone on the high school basketball court. My future Golden Gloves champion seems stuck in a black, inarticulate funk. His head's hung low and he's dragging his private agony around like chains. His sadness seems to be filling the entire gymnasium. I remember those 18-year-old feelings. After I lost in the Golden Gloves finals and let Dom down, I was so downhearted that when I went to bed, thinking of guns was the only thing that relaxed me.

After lunch, I spot Tyrone again, strolling in the hallway. He's sporting a new head-treatment—a multi-colored, Peruvian skullcap with tassels.

"Nice hat," I lie. "Where'd you get it?"

"The city."

"Fourteenth Street?"

"How'd you know?"

"Lucky guess. Wish you'd attend school instead of hanging out on 14th Street. Remember what you once said?"

"What?"

"You said you were my next Golden Gloves champ."

"You layin' a guilt-trip on me?"

Maybe I am. "Hey, let me buy you lunch," I say. "I'll tell you a story about myself."

We sit in the student cafeteria and I tell him what a knucklehead I was in high school. How Crazy Steve ended up on The Bowery suffocating in vomit. How Tommy, at 27, hung himself in jail. God rest their souls.

I tell Tyrone about my street fights and my demented stepfamily. My 35 fights. Maybe I'm revealing too much, but I want him to know he's not the only kid with problems.

He quietly chews his hamburger.

"Once my stepfather tried to kill my mom," I say.

He looks up.

"With scissors. He came home one night…"

"Drunk?"

I nod. "They started arguing in their bedroom. Next morning I see a hole in their mattress. I put my finger in and it went all the way down."

"I'm sorry, Coach," he says, sucking ketchup off his forefinger. "Where was your real father at?"

"Writing songs."

Tyrone is nodding. "Sorry you had to go through that," he says. "Fathers suck."

Monday, March 23:

Tyrone Crooks comes! He's mellow and mute. He's wrapping his hands with yellow gauze and eagerly pulling on his bag gloves with his teeth. Later, I watch him thrash his reflection in the cracked mirror. At the end of a round, I extend my hand. "How you doing?"

"Not good," he murmurs.

"Why?"

He shrugs.

Tyrone's a mystery. Except for when I glimpse him in school, I only see him for an hour and a half—when he trains. He's a big fat question mark. To be with Tyrone is to be dazzled by his raw talent, confused by his secrecy, seduced by his potential, stunned by his stupidity and alarmed by his volatility. In a way, he's a physiological freak. He's gifted with superior speed, fast-twitch muscle, and exceptional anticipation, but comes packaged with such an unfortunate, self-defeating personality.

Is he a dormant volcano ready to explode? A criminal? My future Golden Gloves Champ? Someone once said, *We are who we are when we are alone.* I'd love to secretly follow him down to 14th Street.

Tuesday, March 24:

Tyrone doesn't show. But Caveman Kirk does.

He stomps in wearing his filthy, landscaping uniform covered with wet grass. He has hat hair.

"It's drismal outside," he mutters.

Kirk's a mess. His facial twitch is worsening. Sometimes I can read a guy's face, when he has no *oomph*. Kirk is a nice young man unable to fight without hurting anyone but himself.

Where's Tyrone?

Friday, March 27:

Smiling, Sing-Sing walks into my classroom and hands me a copy of *The Orange*, the White Plains High School student newspaper. Inside is a full-page article devoted to my boxing gym. There's a great photo showing Blacks, Whites and Latinos all working out together. It's a beautiful mix of humanity, that you don't find in too many places.

Unfortunately, later, during 5th period, Sing-Sing finds me in the teacher's room. "Well, Coach Wood, I have disturbing news. It's about one of your flowers."

"Who?"

"You can't guess…?"

10

His Penis is Lethal

I never stole anything that didn't begin with 'A':
A car. A truck. A purse.

—Rocky Graziano, on his juvenile
delinquent days

"…Tyrone Crooks. A few weeks ago, in Manhattan, he *allegedly* raped a 29-year-old woman. That boy's a handsome devil, but his penis is lethal."

Crooks finally cracked.

"You really like him, don't you?" she says.

I think about that for a while. "Honestly, I'm not so sure anymore. He's so emotionally uncoordinated, so socially sick. I thought boxing might iron him out, touch him somehow."

"Is that why you boxed? To get ironed out? Is that why you hooked into him?" she asks.

"Maybe." In a way, Tyrone *is* me. This past week, I read his

Confidential File in the guidance office. He was alcoholic-dependent at birth and suffered broken ribs as an infant by his drug-addicted stepfather. He never actually got to know his real father—he disappeared years ago. All his life the poor kid had school problems, from throwing up in kindergarten to being dumped into Warwick School for Boys at 14.

Do I like him? I pause to think about this question. It's not the first time I've thought about it, of course. "I've known since the very first day I saw Tyrone that that could've been me if I hadn't met Dom Bufano."

She nods.

"Sing-Sing," I say softly. "My brother and I grew up niggers in our stepfather's house. But I flourished in the basement punching bags."

Suddenly, there's a tentative knock on the teacher's room door.

"Come in!" calls Sing-Sing.

Matt, my 4th period student, sticks his head into the room. "Great article, Mr. Wood! I'm joining!" He bolts out.

Sing-Sing shakes her head. "Peter, do you know who gave me chocolates last week?"

I look over at the long-haired creep, Todd Rapier, reading *The Wall Street Journal* in the corner. "Him?"

"No."

"Who?"

She exhales. "I believe this person has been trying to bed me."

"Who?"

"You can't guess?"

"Tell me."

She grins, "You'll be shocked…"

11

The Soft Eight-Year-Old
Living Beneath
My Skin

**_Boxing is probably the best and most
individual lifestyle you can have in
society without being a criminal._**

—Randy Neuman, New Jersey heavyweight

Friday, April 3:

"...Tyrone. He said _we'd make beautiful babies._"

The teachers' room door yawns opens.

"Boxing's a shitty sport," says the varsity hockey coach, placing his coffee mug on the table beside us. His orange sweatpants are clouded with chalk dust.

"Pete, I don't want to interrupt you, especially while you're flirting with Ms. Tu, but Tyrone Crooks is yours, right?"

I nod.

"Well, I happen to like him. He's very helpful in my gym class. But yesterday he tells me _to go jump in a lake._"

"That boy's a noble savage," says Todd Rapier, ambling over. He's the thirty-year-old Harvard know-it-all, with a dirty-blond ponytail and gaunt vegetarian face. "Don't judge the young lad too harshly. He comes from the mud of civilization."

Teachers in the room moan—we've all heard his *shtick* a million times.

"Nice way to talk about a student," I say.

"That's the rub," he says. "This boy is no *student*. How is he as a *pugilist*?"

I want to slap his puss. I see his tortoise-shell eyeglasses skidding across the floor. But I'm not a quick or agile thinker, so I stand up to leave.

"Tell me, Peter, when boxing, what's the best way to bite an opponent, with canines or incisors?" he asks.

"Rapier, it would be a great pleasure to punch you a new fucking asshole," I say, almost. Instead, I'm professional, I gather my papers and mutter, "Screw you."

"Relax, my good man!" He extends his arms in a gesture of innocence. "I'm only playing with you!"

I walk out.

I got my ass verbally kicked. I hate that. I should've put up a fight. But I didn't because, well, I know myself. I'd s-s-stutter and end up his verbal chew-toy like with my stepfather. Fuck me. Deep down, I'm a fleer, not a fighter. I'm Herbie Pish—a soft, inarticulate, fleeing teenager. The worst part? Sing-Sing was there.

I'll get him one day. You watch.

Tuesday, April 7:

"Todd was rude," says Sing-Sing, popping her head into my classroom.

I look up from the play I'm reading, *The Miracle Worker* by William Gibson.

"But he means well," she adds.

I stare in disbelief. "Sing-Sing, you don't know him. Rapier punches everyone."

"Todd has opinions."

The pencil I'm holding snaps. It's always bothered me, how smart, nimble-minded guys eat up athletic guys—it makes them feel more athletic.

"He can't help it if he's smart," she says.

"Yeah, he's smart. He ass kisses every administrator when they're in the room and badmouths them as soon as they walk out the door."

"You jealous?"

"Jealous?" I scoff. Secretly, I'm much worse. I'll never admit it, but I'm frightened of him. Of his wit. He walks into the room and I'm eight-years-old again, back in my stepfather's kitchen, nervously twisting dinner napkins in my lap.

Suddenly Todd Rapier strides into my classroom and extends his hand. "Peter, I'm sorry, really sorry, for last Friday. I'm a pompous ass. I apologize."

I see myself leaping up and plunging my broken pencil into his eardrum. He's writhing on the linoleum floor in great pain...

"Okay, you're right. I'm a total asshole," he says. "Peter, as a boxing coach, you do a great job with your boys. You meet them where they are. I could never do that. I admire you." He extends his hand again.

...He's screaming in agony...blood is oozing from his right ear...

"Peter? Shake his hand," says Sing-Sing.

I shake it.

Then he turns to Sing-Sing. "As I mentioned last night at the restaurant, I'm organizing that after-school, academic-enrichment program. One teaching spot's open. Interested?"

She smiles.

"Why don't we step outside and get out of Peter's hair. I'll tell you more about it."

They walk out. I hear him in the hallway languaging things up; soiling the air with his supercilious educational theory. They laugh in a quiet, secretive way that excludes me.

At the restaurant?

12

How Do I Bloom?

I disliked school. I ran away from home a lot, and spent most of my time hiding in subway tunnels.

—Floyd Patterson, the first two-time Heavyweight Champion

Monday, April 13:

Through the teachers room window, Todd Rapier spots Tyrone Crooks and his harem of pretty girls trolling through the school hallway. Tyrone's *fuck-you* hair is sticking up good.

"Why doesn't that boy get a haircut? He looks like a chrysanthemum," he sighs. "We strain in vain to train their brains."

"You *train* an animal," says Robin, an English teacher, "we *educate* children,"

"Exactly my point!" he jabs. "I never attack a student. I attack behavior."

"You're an arrogant snob," quips a math teacher, poking at his calculator.

"*Perhaps…*and I'm quoting here," says Rapier, "*Perhaps everything terrible is in its deepest being something helpless that wants help from us.*"

"W. H. Auden," offers Robin, the 11th grade Honors English teacher.

"You stupid jackass!" I yell, in my mind I gather my papers to leave.

"You know, I think Peter actually wants to punch me," I hear Rapier whisper.

"I wish he would, Malvolio," mutters Robin.

I'm walking down the hall trying to erase *Malvolio* from the blackboard of my mind. Teachers are teaching, students are studenting and custodians are custodianing. Suddenly, I'm ambushed from behind.

Whap!

A wicked kidney shot…Tyrone.

"Is that the hardest you got?"

We grin at each other.

I notice his hostile hairdo. And shiner. It's dripping into a blue-purple puddle beneath his left eye. "Where'd you get the black eye?"

Silence.

"Fourteenth Street?

Silence.

"When can I spar Kirk?" he blurts.

"Look," I say, starting today, I'll credit you $5 a day *if* you train five days straight. On the fifth day you'll box Kirk—and I'll give you $25."

His eyes light up. "Twenty-five bucks?"

"For one week of training."

He hugs me.

"You're a good coach. You believe in me, despite my bullshit."

Wednesday, April 15:

Tyrone's hitting the bags a ton—he's getting ready for Kirk.

He's sporting yet another drastic hairdo with colorful braids and spangles. His spiky dreadlocks stick out like a fright-wig. I'm now totally convinced: his crazy hair is an act of rebellion, some sort of subconscious *fuck you* to me and the civilized world.

"Tyrone!" I call.

He glances up.

"Five on the speed bag!"

He nods.

I notice Tyrone gravitates to the mirror. He's fixated on it. He'll shadowbox in a mirror before he'll hit a bag. Maybe, by looking at his reflection, he feels in touch with himself. Or maybe he wants to punish anyone who reminds himself of himself.

I admit, Tyrone looks good…real good. He has great instincts, ducks after punching, has excellent head movement, beautiful balance and unbelievable fly-squishing speed. He'll kick Kirk's butt and is a cinch to win The New York City Gloves.

But he's a coach's fucking nightmare.

After a grueling one-hour workout Tyrone is sweat-drenched.

"Thanks, Coach," he gasps.

I smile. "You're going to bloom."

"Me?"

"Trust me, you're going to bloom."

He's looking at me like I'm nuts.

Sure, I want to cultivate Tyrone Crooks' confidence. I'd love to help him grow straight *and blossom*. Like Dom Bufano did with me. But maybe a crooked tree is already crooked in the seed before it hits the dirt.

13

My Pinkie Hurts

I did not train as hard as I should have.

—Jackie Turpin, British welterweight in 1972, after being floored 16 times by Antonio Torres

Wednesday, April 29:

"Tyrone just said he's gonna kick my butt," says Kirk, walking into the gym.

That's it! I throw down my *Ring* magazine. "Wanna spar him?"

He nods.

Tyrone's in the game room, adjacent to the gym, shooting pool with Carlos. "Wanna spar?" I ask.

He holds out a limp-wristed hand. "My pinkie hurts."

I grab it and squeeze.

"YO!" he whelps, feigning a punch at my nose. Then, he smirks. "Wanna box a few rounds?"

"I'll knock you out!" he blusters.

"Not *me*."

"Who?"

"Kirk."

"Got no mouthpiece," he grins, trying to wiggle away.

I grin back. "I got one. See you in the gym."

Anxiety coats Tyrone's eyeballs. It's almost like I've invited him to a suicide he doesn't want to commit.

Five minutes later, Tyrone bops in with Carlos.

Kirk is already standing in the ring.

I slap a yellow Ringside headgear onto Tyrone's head. Tyrone's breathing into my face and I smell the McDonald's hamburgers in his stomach. His anxiety is already accelerating and it's metamorphosed into a sickening panic. He isn't hysterical, but he's getting there. He can't stop yapping. This is a higher form of anxiety I'm seeing; an awful kind that foreshadows heart-palpitations and hyperventilation. I saw this behavior once before in a Peekskill High School wrestler. He was hyperventilating, then keeled over and fainted on the mat seconds before his match.

"Quiet!" I snap. "Here's your mouthpiece." I fit an orange-wedge into his mouth and tell him to bite down. In 19th century England, fruit wedges were the first mouthpieces.

He keeps blabbing and I want to yank his tongue out by its roots. "Kick his ass," I say.

"Yeah, kick whitey's ass," whispers Carlos at ringside.

Tyrone's grinning, but his bulging eyes are glassy with fear.

"Fuck him up," grins Carlos.

Tyrone bites down on the orange and looks at Kirk.

I walk over to Kirk who is calmly bouncing up and down. "Remember," I whisper, dabbing extra Vaseline on his red nose, "head movement. Don't let him open your cut. "

"What's wrong with him?" he whispers. "Something's wrong with him, ain't there?"

Clang!

At the beginning of the round, Kirk holds back and Tyrone darts nervously about like a sleek piece of quicksilver—up and down, left and right. He's fast. Super fast. Fast beyond comprehension. He skillfully dodges, dances and flits out of range. With the split-second reflexes of a housefly, he shoots out sneaky, lightning lefts and flashes off quick rights. His tricky feints make Kirk flinch. Tyrone's fists are a blur as they pound into Kirk's face.

At the end of the round, Kirk, grunting with frustration, is swatting vacant air. Tyrone, grinning, is boxing better than humanly possible for someone who never trains.

The tender pink skin on the bridge of Kirk's nose looks okay, but blood's dribbling from his right nostril. I smear more Vaseline on the bridge of Kirk's nose and whisper, "Step it up."

Biting down on his mouthguard hard, he nods.

Clang!

Tyrone runs out. But after thirty seconds he begins gasping, "STOP! I GOTTA STOP! CAN'T BREATHE!"

"You're in the middle of the fucking round! Keep going!" I order.

"Can't breathe!" he whines, dropping his hands.

"Keep going!" yells Carlos.

"Feel my heart!" he cries. "Feel it! *Feel it!*"

I reach into the ring and palm his chest. *Nothing.*

"You ain't got no heart," I mutter.

14

I Ain't Your Dog!

Just about anything I wanted to do.
Nothing constructive.

—Mike Dokes, former WBA Heavyweight
Champion, explaining what he did
during his two-year absence from boxing.

Friday, May 1:
  "I'm quitting," announces Scrawby Roach, walking into my gym office at the end of his workout.

  Ask any boxing coach—the shelf-life of a boxer is short. The euphoria of hitting people wears off quickly—especially if you're the one getting hit.

  "Boxing's just not my thing," he shrugs. "It's not that I'm afraid to get knocked out, it's just that I don't wanna be there when it happens."

  "Too bad," I say, "you throw a wicked left hook."

  "Thanks, Coach. You know something?" he says, "It sucks to be me. I'm an outcast. I never fit in. I thought boxing would help, but even here I'm an outsider. I feel like a pussy each day I step into the ring. I thought boxing might help, but every time I go in, I get scared and hate myself even more."

"Boxing's never fun, is it?"

Then he curls up his upper-lip and bares his two front teeth. "They're fake. When I was ten, my mom brought me to bowling at White Plains Lanes. I stuck my fingers into this blue bowling ball. When I swung it around, it came up and bashed out my front teeth.

I wince.

I feel like quitting boxing too. I'm anxiously ticking off the days on my calendar. Sick of this gym, sick of coaching, sick of boxing.

Twenty-four days remain until summer break.

Fewer boxers are training. Their top three excuses:

1.) I'm studying.
2.) I got a job.
3.) My grandmother died.

15

I Feel...Hunted

Cus D'Amato didn't just prepare his fighters for the ring, he prepared them for life. He helped me make close to a million dollars during my career and do you know how much he took for his cut? Zero! Not a cent. He was an incredible man.

—Jose Torres, Light Heavyweight Champion

Wednesday, May 13:

Tyrone and Carlos are chucking gravel at blackbirds in the gym parking lot. Suddenly, a red Nissan with black tinted glass pulls up. They start bullshitting with the driver. When I'm spotted, the car patches out.

"Who was that?" I ask, strolling over. "Street Mutt?"

"Your mother," chuckles Tyrone, inhaling white wisps of cigarette smoke.

He's giving off such a psychic stench that I want to punch his face. His long arms dangle down, his crazy ghetto hairdo, a Marlboro stuck between his thick lips: Australopithecus with a cigarette.

"See you in the gym," I say.

"What's wit chew? You ain't my daddy," he sneers, full of hostility and disdain.

Instinctively, my arm leaps out. I slap him. I miss.

I remember when I could easily judge a guy's face. "Come closer," I challenge. He's grinning.

Suddenly, remembering I'm *the adult*, I hold up my hands in surrender. "Sorry," I say. But it's too late.

He's spitting out his butt, balling his fists, and walking closer. "Think you can beat me?"

A current of fear runs through me. My testicles are shriveling, my knees are trembling, and I'm tasting sourness in my mouth. "If you're so tough," I say, "why aren't you inside training with Kirk?"

"Fuck you, whitey!" He juts out his chin, daring me.

This time I get him. Almost.

Crooks executes a perfect rockaway—just like I taught. His right fist brushes the hair above my forehead.

My brain is saying attack, but my mouth mutters: "Try that again, I'll beat the shit outta you."

"I'm gonna kill you!" he spits.

I walk away, my knees shaking.

Tonight is Dom Bufano's birthday. I take him to his favorite restaurant—Red Lobster.

During dinner we talk Crooks.

"How do I reach him?" I ask, looking at his dead, milky eye.

"I thought you college boys had all the answers."

"Knock it off, Dom, we've gone through that years ago."

He grins and mulls it over. "First, I'd tell that punk what he needs to hear. I'd tell him point blank: Son, you got a strong body, but a weak mind. I shouldn't have to push you to train." Dom shakes his head. "Fighters don't realize the worry and heartache they put me through. This kid, you reach him by whettin' his appetite. Make him hungry for more. Like I did with you."

I nod.

"Work with him individually and at the end of his workout, ask *On a scale of 1-10 what would you give yourself?* Most fighters love to learn. You did. I couldn't get you outta the gym. Remember? You were a gym rat."

I smile.

"You gotta get this boy to transcend hisself."

"Like you did with me?"

He shrugs sipping his Manhattan clam chowder. "Well, I tried. You had *a calling* but you walked away." He's stirring his soup.

"Yeah, well Praise this stupid kid."

"Doesn't work."

"Then abuse him. Treat him like dirt. He'll get the hint."

"And if he doesn't?"

"Get rid of him," he says, waving his hand, like he was shooing away a housefly.

Dom bites into a sesame seed roll. "You should see the kid I got now. Found him behind A&P pickin' through a trash can scavenging for food." He smiles. "He's white, name's Tony Malzone. Ain't many good white boys around anymore."

As I listen to Dom, all of my usual inadequacy and self-loathing resurfaces. Dom's Svengali and I'm shit. If it weren't for the $20,000, I wouldn't be here. I'm not remotely pure enough to coach kids.

But by dessert I manage to relax and be gentle with myself. By the time I pay the check, I decide I'm just as good a boxing coach as the next psychologically conflicted, guilt-ridden neurotic.

At home, the phone is ringing.

"C-Coach, it's me, B-Bobo. You heard about Crooks?"

"No."

"H-He was shooting pool in the game-room. Some kid s-suckered him and Crooks beat him up. Kid went to the hospital all bloody."

"You see it?"

"Yeah."

"Did Crooks tuck his jaw to his chest?"

"Huh?"

"Did he tuck his jaw to his chest?"

"Yeah, I think."

"Did he throw combinations?"

"You be b-buggin', Coach!"

"Well, did he?"

"Yeah," chuckles Bobo.

"How'd he look?"

"Boy's crazy q-quick."

I wonder if Crooks pinned his elbow to his stomach. I'll ask tomorrow.

16

Boxing's the *Last* Thing That Little Mutant Needs

If a boxer ever went crazy as Nijinsky all the wowsers in the world would be screaming 'punch-drunk'. Well, who hit Nijinsky? And why isn't there a campaign against ballet? It gives girls thick legs.

**—A. J. Liebling, in the introduction to
*The Sweet Science***

Tuesday, May 26:

"Tyrone Crooks is in the psych ward," says Malcolm. "His mother committed him last night."

Disappointment, anger, sadness and relief, wash over me.

No more Golden Glove Champion…No more death threats.

"He stopped by my office this morning."

"You just said he's in a psych ward."

"Released this morning. A doctor suggested we enter him in our automotive program."

Shit.

My boxing program is falling apart. Another malcontent stuck a metal thumbtack in my light bag last night. When Kirk picked it out, the bag shriveled like a prune. This time, it couldn't possibly be Tyrone.

Who?

Wednesday, June 3:

Kirk's poor nose is getting flatter and the flesh on his top lip is purple and puffy. He's becoming battle scarred and I'm reminded of Randy Sandy, a pro middleweight who slurred his words because of the brain damage he sustained while sparring in a tough Philadelphia gym.

Stuttering Bobo rolfs Kirk's nose bone for two rounds. But after round four, it's Kirk who's standing. Bobo, exhausted, sinks to the canvas. Lying on his back, Bobo's gulping air like a dying fish. *"I's dead,"* he gasps. After landing so many punches on Kirk's nosebone, I'm sure he is. I inspect Kirk's cut, swab out his swollen nostrils, and towel off the two red trickles running down.

"You're getting dangerously good, " I say, looking at his battered face.

"Ya think so?" he smiles.

"Bobo's a rough kid."

"What do you think about me entering The Gloves this year?"

I'm looking at his red potato face that's slowly being rearranged. It's pitiful. Kirk's slowly becoming me. The boxing virus has entered his bloodstream. Could he win The Gloves? He's getting pretty damn good for someone who has no talent. "Let's take one day at a time, okay?"

Thursday, June 4:

Early this morning, while walking towards the school entrance, I spot Tyrone Crooks smoking a butt in the faculty parking lot. He's standing beside the same red Nissan with black tinted windows. "How ya doing, Coachy?" he calls.

Will my tires be slashed?
Or will I?

A colleague joins me walking towards the school entrance. "Did you hear what that boy told Mrs. Grusko last week? He blurted out 'I'll beat you like cake mix'."

"No, it was 'I'll *eat* you like cake mix'," says another teacher joining us.

Within thirty seconds I'm hearing: *conduct disorder, A.D.D.,* and *mentally defective.*

"How's his boxing therapy going?" asks a voice.

It's Sing-Sing.

I glance back at Tyrone smoking his cigarette. I think about Tyrone's beleaguered mind

marbled with all of the essential ingredients that lead to a championship title. What garlic is to salad, insanity is to boxing. But with Tyrone, it just isn't happening.

"Maybe I was wrong," I admit.

Sing-Sing's eyes are sad. "You're becoming a big joke in school, you know. Everyone's laughing behind your back."

"Are *you* laughing?"

Her stare doesn't waver. "I've told you a million times—boxing isn't the answer. Boxing is your private little mud puddle. It's time to grow up."

She looks back at Tyrone who's blowing smoke rings. She shakes her head. "Just look at that."

"What happened to providing miracles for kids?" I ask.

"Fisticuffs is the *last* thing that child needs." It's Todd Rapier, striding from behind. His blond ponytail is fluttering in the breeze as he wraps his arm around Sing-Sing's waist. "Your boxing prodigy sleeps in my study hall, but I prefer it that way. I don't mean to be harsh, Peter, but I wish I could do a urinalysis of his mind to see what's up there."

"Todd! Stop!" interrupts Sing-Sing. "You promised."

"Peter, do you know what *maf* is? *Maf* is *math.*" He points to a small scar above his eye. "A few years back, I tried to correct a student's pronunciation, and he attacked me. All I was trying to do was educate him. Then—*Wham!*"

"I'd love to shake his hand."

"Actually, you know him. Willy Bullens…Street Mutt?"

My heart skips a beat.

"Peter, I was once like you—I felt sorry for these little cretins and thought they could be saved." He shakes his head. "Sorry."

"I'm afraid Todd's right," says Sing-Sing, entering the school.

***

In the gym, the heavybag crashes to the floor. The metal loop breaks while Tiger Green, the pro middleweight, pounds it. It was bound to snap, sooner or later.

While Tiger and I re-hang it, I overhear Kirk and Herbie Pish arguing in the locker room: "Herbie, beans are *not* meat."

"Yes, they are."

"No. Beans are vegetables."

"No," says Herbie, "Just like a bat is a bird *and* a mouse, beans are a protein *and* a vegetable."

"No, Herbie, beans're *vegetables*. And vegetables're vegetables."

"No."

"Look," says Kirk, "if you was on death-row because you murdered someone, what would you request for a last meal? *Beans?*"

"Are you mental? I wouldn't kill nobody. Except Scrawby, of course."

"Just answer my question," says Kirk.

I hear Herbie sniffing his fingers. "Well, I'd order something real expensive, like sushi."

"And for dessert?" asks Kirk.

"Strawberry shortcake…with chocolate ice cream. And I'd want it to be a *wedding* cake—*a wedding to myself*—with an electric chair on top. But no doll sitting in it, just the chair."

"Anything to drink?"

"Doctor Pepper, no ice." Then he adds, "When I do die, I'll

94

derive some comfort knowing that I'll never see your red punchy face again."

Kirk laughs. "Herbie, you been sniffing too much glue."

In the middle of the night, the phone rings. "Hello?"

"Pete, it's Malcolm. Bad news."

"What."

"Tyrone was arrested.

17

There But For the Grace of Boxing Go I

***I was in handcuffs. I was under arrest. I remember
there was this old lady looking at me, and I could
tell she felt sorry for me, and she didn't know but
all I wanted to do was take her purse***

***—Mike Tyson, as a young juvenile delinquent
recalling an episode in his youth***

Friday, June 5:

Westchester County Jail is a red brick insane asylum. A fifteen-foot-high Cyclone fence, reinforced on top with spiraling steel razor-wire, surrounds it. And my champion is sitting inside.

I'm staring into his angry face. "What are you in for?"

He avoids my question. "This place sucks," he mutters. "I'm in here with murderers and thieves. They'll slit your throat. But I gotta make the best of a shit situation. The goddamn authority don't care about nothin'…"

Here's the end of the line for one more Mike Tyson wannabe.

"…then I wake up and eat breakfast, they never serve me enough damn food. It's disgustin', they just don't care…"

That's my tough Golden Gloves champ bitching. I imagine him supping shoulder to shoulder with Alexander Solzhenitsyn, both hunched over dirty wooden bowls slurping dead soup.

He's affecting a sniffling sense of authority. He looks over his shoulder at the armed guards standing against the wall. My little convict. He's beginning to speak with the rote manner of a tour guide. His lips curl like he thinks he's some genius.

"Why you in here?" I repeat.

No answer.

I listen to his phony maturity. What he's absorbing most deeply in jail isn't any sort of wisdom but arrogance, a cynical self-serving bravado and a twisted vision of the world that makes him feel better about himself.

What did I ever see in him?

"…I wanna join the Job Corps, but at my interview, I lost my temper…So now I's sittin' here insteada the damn Job Corps…"

Crooks isn't crying in the traditional sense, it's more of a macho blubbering—the worst kind. I wouldn't call Crooks a mamma's boy, but like many boys, he's hooked into mama, big-time.

"…If she died tomorrow, I'd be going to her funeral wearing handcuffs. Who wants to go to their mom's funeral wearing handcuffs?"

"You blew it, man. You really blew it," I say.

"Yeah, you right." Then, for the first time, he looks squarely at me. "I'm reading the Bible. But it makes me feel guilty. Says if you bad to your family, it shortens your life."

"What verse?"

He shrugs and looks down at his paper shoes.

"Tyrone, what did you do?"

Silence.

"…I'm getting my G.E.D., but school's *whack*. It's just a big room, so I take my books and read in my…room. I pass readin', social studies and maf."

Maf.

I nod.

"Probation officer's still tryin' to get me into The Job Corps, though. Depends on my next interview. But there's one subject he keeps bringin' up…" A dark anger twists his face. His eyes dart around the room; it looks like he wants to flee or fight something that's buried deep inside, yet—at the same time—lying close to the surface.

"Tell me, Tyrone…"

"…My father." He glances at me and looks away. "Coach, I'm sorry things didn't work out with you and me. Maybe next time."

I look at Tyrone's confused face. Despite its anger, it's still a handsome face. I'm listening to his ridiculous rap and, to an extent, I sympathize with the punk. *There but for the grace of boxing go I.*

Crooks is destroying himself.

Is there no way out of the mind? asks Sylvia Plath in one of her last desperate poems. I thought Crooks' way was boxing. I was wrong.

"…So, now I'm a janitor and sweep garbage for $15 a week. Damn!…"

I get the feeling that he's deriving some sort of unconscious joy from his assumed victimization and righteous anger. Erich Fromm said, *A criminal is a creator gone wrong; those who cannot create will always destroy.*

I think of prison dust. Forty percent of household dust and lint, I'm told, is sloughed-off human skin. Then I visualize Alexander Solzhenitsyn, Tyrone Crooks and Mike Tyson, side-by-side, sweeping human skin.

"Cut the shit, Tyrone, why you in here?"

He looks down at the desk. "Bitches."

The blind areas in Tyrone's brain are many. I look into his eyes and, somewhere, I still believe, deeply buried behind that thick skull, is creativity, intelligence, and a capacity to love. Maybe him sitting in a jail cell is best. Maybe he'll slough off some poisonous skin and regenerate. Maybe one day he'll wake up.

It's dark outside, and as I walk toward my smashed, vandalized car gray heavyweight clouds are lumbering silently overhead. Inside my head I'm feeling a small scratching...it's in the corner of my mind...it's word. This word has been crawling around the perimeter of my skull for awhile now. It's upside down and backwards... It's flipping from side to side and is all jumbled up...

...Driving home, I realize I still want to lift Crooks up, hold him, and help him stop being gnawed by his own self-destruction. I step into my apartment, and that little word is still crawling through my skull. I walk upstairs, and it starts tiptoeing...now thrashing... clawing inside my head, stuck, trying to escape.

It's two words.

It's only when I'm naked in the shower that they scramper out...*Forgiveness... Mother.*

18

The Key

"This ain't the last round, Sam."
"It is for you."

—*Exchange between old-time heavyweight*
Sam "The Boston Tar Baby" Langford and
Jack Thompson, when Langford extended
his glove at the start of the seventh round.
One punch later, Thompson was unconscious.

Friday, June 12, 1998:
    Today's my last day coaching—until September. Kirk Sloboda
stuns everyone by bloodying Bobo's nose with a right hand
counter. *WHAP!*
    I'm proud of Kirk. He's worked hard. But I continue to be wor-
ried about the welfare of his face.
Packing up at the end of the day, I'm proud of all my kids. At
first, they resembled dirty, dried-up tubers—gnarled with no visible signs of life. Each day, I watched them sprout and come alive
like vegetables growing in the soft soil of the gym. In a way, I feel
like a gardener walking among his plants. Except Tyrone Crooks.

At 6:30, everyone's gone.

Alone, I look at the fight posters on the red brick walls. The scorching gym air is grief-like. The gym is a decaying corpse with no heartbeat. It's *drismal.*

But what aches me most is Sing-Sing: Why didn't I put up a fight?

I gaze up at the old dead champions on the brick wall: Jack Johnson, Jack Dempsey, Joe Louis, Rocky Marciano, Kid Chocolate and a teenage Dom Bufano squaring off with Sugar Ray Robinson. "Good-bye," I whisper.

I flick off the lights.

"Hey!" growls a voice. "Where you think you're going?"

It's Street Mutt. He's standing in the middle of the ring wearing black trunks and red boxing shoes. The blue gloves on his hands are identical to the ones stolen from the gym—so are the red shoes.

"How'd you get in here?"

He laughs.

"Get out!" I bark. I quickly search for my car key. "I'm locking up."

"Lookin' for this?" He holds up a key. *My* key.

He takes off a glove, drops the key inside, and shoves his fist back in. "Come get it."

"Those gloves, and shoes, are mine."

"Well, come get 'em!" he grins.

I slip through the ring ropes. "Gimmee."

"Gimmee your job!" he spits, walking closer. "I'm The Golden Gloves Champ, not you!"

"So that's your problem!" I say.

"Why do whitey always get hired?" he blurts, inching closer.

I hold out my hand. "Give me my key."

He smacks it away, then throws three swift jabs at my face; the last one catches my nose.

Blood trickles onto my chest.

"I told you I'd fuck you up! Remember?" He starts dancing to my right. "Let's do it!"

If I were clever, I'd talk my way out, but in situations like these, my mind always clamps shut. *Peter, throw the first punch,* whispers Dom Bufano.

I rush, dip low and chuck a left hook. Miss. Street Mutt counters with a sharp one-two. My neck jolts back and I see white explosions. He's on me quick, slamming home punches. I duck, but he's too fast and corners me with a vicious four-punch combination. His fists plunge into my face and soft stomach. I hang on, gasping. He rips a hard hook into my eye and I feel an old cut reopen; blood trickles down my cheek. He cuts loose with another flurry, then cracks my head open with a head butt. More blood.

"C'mon, you the boxing coach! You tough!" he sneers. He proceeds to nail me with a sneak right over the top.

I try to be tough. I rush in throwing a left hook—right upper-cut combination, but it's wild. I throw a double left-hook—he parries both. I throw a right cross-right uppercut combination—miss. My blood is covering my chest, canvas and blue gloves. I am pitiful.

"You suck!" he laughs. He thumps his gloves together, lets out a crazy howl, and attacks. I can tell he's having a good time.

I bob beneath his lead right and clinch. I'm holding on to one massive piece of flowing, fibrous muscle. I clinch tight, but after a million jailhouse pushups Street Mutt's much too strong. He muscles loose and splats a right-cross flush on my mouth. An excruciating pain jolts from my mouth to the top of my head. Something sharp and jagged is on my tongue. My tooth. The sonofabitch cracked my front tooth.

He's punching me at will. I stumble and am about to get knocked out. I have to do something quick…

…I spit my tooth into his face.

He's laughing.

I grab tight and bury my head into his chest. My mouth opens. I'm about to bite down on his nipple, but I can't do it. There's not enough animal in me.

"You suck!" he snickers.

Have to do something quick—real quick…

…"Crooks!" I gasp, looking at the door.

Street Mutt's eyes dart to the door. I heave a desperate left-hook—
my legs, hips, elbow and shoulder all behind it.

CRACK!

Down he slumps—flat on his back—out cold. Some guys don't
have a good jaw—he's one. I could've counted to one hundred, he
wasn't getting up. Don't know if it was quick thinking but, whatever
it was, I sure saved myself.

I yank off his glove and grab my key.

My key inside a boxing glove.

I don't kick his head or anything, even though I think about it for
a second. I just pick up my cracked tooth from the canvas, flick off
the lights, and leave.

ROUND 2

"A Resignation Letter"

Maybe I'm getting too old for this.
Maybe I'd better start looking for
something else to do.

—Dwight Muhammad Qawi, after losing to
Evander Holyfield

Thursday, June 17:
  Street Mutt was arrested on Sunday. Thanks to him, I've now got a new front tooth. But I'm glad I got beat up. I used these kids chasing my youth. And to make $20,000.
  But no more.
  I'm sitting at my kitchen table, eating a soft cheese sandwich, writing my resignation letter, effective December 1st.

"Oh, God!" colleagues gasp, when I report back to work. "Your face! What happened?"
  I tell them I stumbled while rock-climbing up the Mohonk Mountains.

August…September…October:

I'm walking the well-worn path of the boxing coach, barking instructions with dutiful attention. But I'm a phony. I'm trying to be absorbed by my fighters' progress, but there's no spark. I'm cheating these kids. I should've resigned in June. This ugly, sweltering gym's killing me. It's blood money. I don't even have the necessary energy to smile or imagine their success. I trudge to the heavybag, to the lightbag, to the mirror, to the ring. I'm just faking it.

I'm a parasitic worm crawling in the mud of boxing.

My resignation letter is waiting…December 1st…166 days.

Round 3

THE MAIN EVENT

The difference between involvement and commitment is a ham and egg sandwich—the chicken is involved, the pig is committed.

—Gerry Cooney, heavyweight contender

Monday, November 16:

Kirk's flat nose got flatter that round. Dom's A&P trash-eating scavenger, Tony Malzone, is slapping him around good. Not hurting him, just humiliating him. Poor Kirk. He's getting hit with every punch. In boxing, everyone is on someone else's menu, and Kirk continues to be on the lower end of the food chain. It's disgusting.

I hope, with all my heart, in heaven there is no boxing.

After sparring two rounds with Kirk, two with Stuttering Bobo and two with Tiger, The Scavenger's mouth hangs open with fatigue.

"Coach, I'll fight him now," whispers Cockeye, my new 300-pound heavyweight. Cockeye reminds me of someone wanting to creep onto a battlefield after the battle is over to shoot the wounded. "Cockeye, you're a soft, flabby piece of poultry. At your weight it probably takes a lot just to rest," I think. "Okay, tomorrow," I grimace.

I hate boxing.

At the end of the day, in the locker room, Kirk is slumped in front of a mirror. I overhear him talking to his red dented face. "I suck, I suck, I suck..."

It's *drismal.*

I resign in 14 days...

Tuesday, November 17:

"My name's Dino Lazaro...I'm twenty-one...Have over 100 amateur fights."

I look at his straight nose and perfect white teeth. No way that face saw 100 fights.

"Fought in Lunar Gym...Manhattan," he says, softly.

He's a handsome boy with dark brown eyes and straight black hair. He stands 5' 9".

We shake. His hands are small and delicate. One hundred fights? Hey, who hasn't fought 100 fights in his bedroom mirror, pretending to beat up Jack Dempsey, Mike Tyson, or the neighborhood bully?

When this Dino kid steps onto the floor in his gold satin trunks and begins punching the heavybag, he isn't pretending. His muscles are popping. He's diesel.

I'm looking at his broad shoulders and slender waist. "You lift weights?"

"Three times a week...Holyfield's routine."

Weights and boxing, traditionally, don't mix. Lifting heavy weights bulks you up and slows you down. But this kid's fast and flexible. And he hits like a demon, so why not? (My buddy, Vito Antuofermo—a New York Golden Gloves Champ and Middleweight Champion of the World—lifted weights, too.)

I'm watching him punish the bag. I can tell he wants to impress me; on the floor around the heavybag are quarter-sized sweat drops. I'm not exaggerating.

I notice Kirk eyeballing Dino. Poor Kirk's sitting there, taking it all in. He shakes his head in disgust. I look at his two black eyes and swollen nose from yesterday. "My shoulder," he murmurs, kneading it.

Kirk, I can almost feel your disappointment. Despite all of your hard, honest work, you're not really improving. "Kirk," I say, "if a guy had me down in an alley, beating the hell out of me, who do you think I'd holler for, you or that sissy Malzone kid?"

Kirk smiles glumly. "Thanks, Coach."

But I don't think Kirk's shoulder is what's really bothering him, or his swollen nose or black eyes or his fat lip whicj has faded into a yellowy green. I think it has more to do with yesterday. Then today, seeing this new boy.

"Kirk, you're a nice kid trapped in a stupid boxing gym. And you're becoming a slut for punishment. The only person you're hurting is yourself," I want to say.

I'm only too happy to give him his way out: "Kirk, can I tell you a secret? This boxing shit is stupid. It's a lousy sport. I, honestly, don't see why you do it."

I can see his relief. No more welts, bloody noses or black eyes. "I tried, Coach."

When Kirk walks out the door, I never see him again.

Kirk, I hope one day you realize you're lucky. You just don't have enough vindictive malice. Jimmy Cannon, the protégé of Damon Runyon, once said of Rocky Marciano: *Rocky stood out like a rose in a garbage dump.* That's you, Kirk.

Thursday, November 19:

Dino points to a photo of a young black boxer taped to the brick wall. "Fought him."

"No kidding?" says Tiger.

"Seven times." He swivels his thick neck. "Lost first three, beat him next four."

That evening, I call Dom. "Do me a favor. Bring Tony up again. I have a middleweight. Name's Lazaro."

"Bring him down to my gym. Let's see what he's got."

"He'll box Tony?"

"I'll see what I can do, honky!" he hollers. "Be content with the crumbs I throw you!"

My resignation letter goes in the drawer.

Monday, November 23:

Sitting on the concrete floor in his jockstrap, Dino starts talking in clipped sentences. "My dad was Puerto Rican, mom Italian...One summer we flew to Puerto Rico...a boxing camp...I boxed at 79 pounds...Then dad died...alcohol...mom died, too...stopped boxing."

He stands and slips into his gold satin boxing trunks.

"Where you work?" asks Cockeye, squeezing himself into his gray sweatpants.

"Westchester Airport...baggage loader."

I look at the bloody bandage taped to his shin. "What happened?"

"Box fell...bad things happen to me."

Wednesday, November 25:

"I wanna enter The Gloves," says Dino softly.

I look at him hard. At twenty-one, he's a perfect blend of youth and maturity. Plus, he's naturally strong, has great moves, and, maybe, the proper attitude.

And he's a converted southpaw. Like me. This gives him an advantage because you trick your opponent into focusing in on your weak hand—your right. *The best liar wins*—Dom's motto.

Hey, entering the Golden Gloves is radical. It's one of the most bizarre, yet wonderful, things a kid can do because it leads to self-awareness. Especially if he can punch.

"You do, huh?" I ask.

He nods.

When I was a kid, all you had to do was say "Golden Gloves" and my nose would bleed. Now I get indigestion.

I've only known this kid for a few days. Will he work consistently? Can he re-enter this religion called boxing? Can he live in an inspired condition for three months? Can he electrify that primitive part of his brain and become grotesque? Does he have *The Calling*?

I see the quarter-sized sweat drops on the floor. My pores once spit out those sweat drops.

"Come here," I say. We walk over to my *Fighter's Photo Gallery* on the brick wall. I show him snapshots of Crooks. Then Kirk. "See him? You scared him out of the gym last week. He recently bought all new boxing gear, but once he saw you, his shoulder started hurting." I wonder if this is going to happen to him the first time something goes wrong. "If you want to enter The Gloves, go home and do some soul-searching."

Five rounds later, Dino approaches me, lacquered with sweat. "I know that

Feeling…being scared."

I smile. Honesty is rare in a fighter.

"Stopped fighting at 11. Now it's my dream."

"Your dream. Or your father's?"

He looks away.

"It's been a tough ten years, huh?"

He nods. "Foster homes…Brooklyn. Queens. Manhattan. Rockland."

"How'd you hear about my gym?"

"By accident," he shrugs.

There are no accidents.

"Tried a gym in Haverstraw. But the Dominicans and me…," I shakes his head.

"Tried other places, but…" He shrugs.

This kid's beginning to get interesting. I sense that we have much in common. Like unfinished business and residual shitdetox."

"Detox? You? For what?" asks Tiger, tying his shoe.

"Cocaine...heroin."

I'm floored. My older brother shot heroin. He was dead on the bathroom floor when police found him.

"I'm clean now," he says, throwing a few punches.

Clean for how long? But it isn't the right time to dig. I want to ask so many questions: What makes a guy stick a needle in his arm? Who introduced you to drugs? What does heroin feel like? "Well," I say, "welcome back."

I'm watching Dino smack the heavybag. The thump and thwack of his fists is the sound of something important being accomplished. How often do you *hear* skill? I find it very gratifying, especially after learning what I have just learned. Art begins in a wound, an imperfection.

After a hot, grueling one-hour workout, I take him aside. "Entering The Gloves is a total commitment. I don't even know if *I* can commit to it.

I look into his stoic face. It's a good-looking face; chiseled and determined. Can he do it? Can he swallow the chaos? Most people can't remain loyal to a single goal for long; it's too narrow and stressful. After one or two fights, would Dino's Golden Gloves *dream* become drudgery?

"I'm dead serious," he says

So was Tyrone.

1

THE WARM-UP

Philadelphia is not a town. It's a jungle. They don't have gyms there, they have zoos. They don't have sparring sessions, they have wars. "

—Angelo Dundee, Muhammad Ali's trainer

Monday, December 14:

Dino and I walk into Bufano's Gym in the bowels of Jersey City. It's a dirty, deranged room full of hostility. It's a stink, an infection, a dream. Dom's been here for 30 years.

There's a problem: No Tony Malzone. Sure, I'm peeved, but I sort of let it go because for a kid, just traveling to another gym, in itself, is a good learning experience. It's a gut check.

Dino suits up, laces on his 10-ounce gloves and begins smacking my hand-pads. He throws a series of impressive double left hooks. "C'mon, harder!" I goad. "Hit it off my hand!" (I inch it up, so he can.)

WHAM!

The pad flies off and bangs onto the cement wall. It's a cheap spectacle and a calculated ego-boost. But it's also for Dom's benefit.

"Looks good, don't he?" I grin.

"Not bad," murmurs Dom, feigning nonchalance.

Next, Dino punishes the heavybag for three rounds. It's a 200-pound Ringside water bag—the kind that makes a guy feel like he's hitting human flesh.

Dom's eyes widen. "He throws an over-hand right that'll get a lot of attention," he observes.

Tuesday, December 15:

Dino finally boxes. Two sparring partners are lined up; two rounds with fat Cockeye, and two with Stuttering Bobo. Neither touches a hair on his head. Dino is feinting and creating angles with clever footwork. Man, he's like Ismael Laguna! It's clear that he can take out both guys whenever he wants. Bobo even jumps out of the ring with self-disgust and spits his mouthpiece to the floor.

"Bobo, don't worry," I reassure, "You looked fine." I can't lose Bobo. I have so few fighters and he's invaluable to Dino as his sparring partner.

Cockeye, winded and wheezing, sits on a chair for fifteen minutes to recuperate.

Later, I pat Dino's back and whisper, "You're making these guys do back flips."

That night I can't eat or sleep. I can't breathe. I'm too excited. Dino, I'm positive, you're my New York City Golden Glove Champion.

Wednesday, December 16:

I point to the calendar and show Dino what's ahead—day-by-day—if he enters The Gloves. You have to be concrete with boys.

"Are you up to the challenge?" I ask.

He nods.

"The coaching? The diet?"

He nods.

I point. "January, February, March...For all these weeks? The running? The sparring?"

He nods.

"I'm going to be tough on you," I warn. "If it ain't painful, it ain't boxing."

"Okay," he grins.

"Ever hear of Henry Aaron, the baseball player?" I ask.

He nods.

"He said something that applies to you: If, in your lifetime, you're lucky, you get the chance to do something great. But you have to be prepared to grab it and have the courage to take your best swing." It's corny, but hey.

He smiles a sad smile.

He spars five rounds: two with Cockeye and three with Stuttering Bobo. Again, neither touches a hair on his fucking head.

At the end of his workout, I go up to Dino and ask, "Can you block a left hook?"

He nods.

"Bet you can't." For effect, I slap down $20.

He looks at me weird.

"I'll even *tell* you when I throw it."

"*Left* hook?" he clarifies.

I nod.

We square off.

"Ready?" I feint a quick left to his cheek, then reverse it and slam it to his belly.

POP!

"Told you!" I grin, stuffing the $20 back into my pocket. That was an old Freddy Brown trick. Freddy trained Rocky Marciano in the '50s. He had tricked me in the same manner when I first started.

Monday, December 21:
Why does Dino always sit on the locker room floor? In his mind is he still a 79 pound child?

Dino's ring record, whatever it is, because of the lapse in time, will be wiped clean. He'll qualify for the novice division—a less experienced class—guys with no more than four bouts. (Eligibility rules, year to year, always mysteriously change.)

I play music in the gym: Hip Hop, Rap, Rock. It's another level of reality, more pleasant and tolerable than getting punched in the face. *Pass the Dutchie,* a nice piece of reggae by The Musical Youth, is now playing when the phone rings. It's Kid Corbett. He says he's sorry about trying to steal Tyrone Crooks, but can he come in with one of his pros, Greg Zackar, a 135-pounder, to spar Dino? That's exactly what Dino needs—quality sparring!
So that's how Tyrone's got his black eye!

Tuesday, December 22:
Dino and I drive over the George Washington Bridge to Dom's gym. It's important for a fighter to leave his comfort zone and box in foreign environments. But as soon as Dino takes off his shirt and flexes his muscles, his scheduled sparring-partner chickens out.

Dom rummages around and comes up with a thickly whiskered Latino.
"Who is he?" I ask.
"Don't worry. He'll take it easy," says Dom.
"What's his record?" I ask.
"Trust me."
"Is he open or novice?"
"Trust me."
"How old is he?"
"Relax!" assures Dom. "Carlos'll go easy."
Clang!

Carlos methodically begins to quasi-destroy Dino! He dogs Dino onto the ropes and repeatedly beats him to the punch. He's hitting Dino low, elbowing him and stepping on his feet. Then this *kid* begins shifting lefty and righty, usually an amateurish move, but he's so slick, he can pull it off.

Dino's in over his head. Carlos cannibalizes him. He stops only to blow snot from his nose, then he feasts on Dino again. After two rounds, I've seen enough. "That's it!" I call.

Miserably, Dino steps out.

"Did good, man," I lie.

"I sucked," he mutters.

"Look, you walked into the lion's den and held your own. Remember, this is one of the roughest gyms in Jersey."

"My nuts," winces Dino.

"Yeah, but you got off a few good shots. Remember, you're just starting."

"Feel my forehead," he says. "Got a 102°."

Feels normal.

"Don't worry—you did great." I have to pump him back up—tomorrow he spars a pro.

That night I phone Dom. "Thanks for getting my fighter beat up."

"What're you talkin' about, honky? It was perfect. You got a strong workout."

"Too strong."

"You're so smart you're stupid. Strong workouts teach things you need to know, college boy."

"Can the *college boy* stuff—that was 17 years ago. It was stronger than I wanted."

"Look, Carlos is the toughest dude in my gym."

"Is Tony sparring him?"

Dom chuckles. "Tony? Tony's the strongest dude in my damn gym! Tony *plays* with Carlos!"

He's bullshitting...I know he's bullshitting... I hope he's bullshitting.

Wednesday, December 23:

Dino spars four rounds with Zackar. Dino's head-butted and suffers a minor split lip, but this sometimes comes with good sparring.

"Boy looks strong," nods Kid Corbett. "It's nice to see a kid work hard. Too many pampered punks today. Canzoneri, Zale, Graziano would murder guys today."

"Don't try to steal him," I warn.

"Nah, don't worry," he chuckles.

I dig into my dufflebag, pull out a vial of ginseng. "Here, Dino, drink this. It heals cut lips."

Dino is my new champion. I smell it. I buy him multi-vitamins and write down his address so I can drop off a box of Sunkist oranges. I also write him a study list:

1. **You're headhunting—punch more to the body.**
2. **Feint to make openings.**
3. **Establish your jab.**
4. **Sit down on your punches—you're punching at 60% capacity.**
5. **Work on** *Technique,* *Stamina* **and** *Power.*

Before he leaves, I hand him a stopwatch. "Your Christmas present. Run three six-minute miles."

"That's fast."

"Yeah, well that's what I ran. Merry Christmas."

He nods, zipping up his brown leather jacket.

I lie. I never ran three six-minute miles. Nowhere close. I plodded along with heavy construction boots.

"Where you spending Christmas?" I ask.

He shrugs. "Home."

Kid's not much of a talker. I feel horrible. No mother. No father. No family.

Thursday, December 24, Christmas Eve:

Tonight I buy Dino a real Christmas gift—*Somebody Up There Likes Me,* Rocky Graziano's autobiography. Inside, I write: *Merry Christmas to the next Middleweight Golden Gloves Champ!*

I drive down Lincoln Avenue, a pretty tree-lined street to his rented apartment in Silver Lake, a respectable middleclass neighborhood with small well-manicured white houses. I want to hand him his Christmas gift. Maybe we'll eat dinner together. We're both alone.

I park my car and walk to his front door. Inside, I hear a soft hammering. And a muffled groaning. "Awgh, you asshole!"

Bang!

"Awgh, you suck!"

Bang!

"Awgh, you asshole!"

Bang!...

2

THE SIGN IN

Training fighters is like trying to catch a fish.
It's technique, not strength.

—Angelo Dundee

… "Aargh!"

Bang!…

Someone's heat is banging on the wall? Or floor? Or getting punched? The anguish in the tortured voice gives me the willies. I'm not supposed to be hearing this. I stuff the book in his mailbox and leave.

Was it Dino?

Monday, January 4:

I'm very concerned. Is something wrong with Dino? When he undresses, sitting on the floor, I look for red welts on his head. I see none.

Dino, you're scaring me.

Each day for the past two weeks, he's been moving like a champ in the ring, but he's moving alone. Reminds me of the standup comic who joked, *I'm great in bed, unless someone's in there with me.* But this isn't funny. Dino's scaring away potential sparring partners. Zackar comes only once in a while, and that isn't enough. Where's Tiger? I have Fat Cockeye and Stuttering Bobo. That's it. Not counting Tiger, my boys have a grand total of five fights. That's nothing compared to most New York clubs that have hundreds! We need pro fighters in here, dammit! Amateurs need a gym where they can observe, mimic, and learn from pros. Dino needs quality sparring if he's going to win the title.

Meanwhile, Fat Cockeye lumbers in clutching a clear plastic bag full of bloody chunks of hairy meat. He drops it on the table. "I shot a deer in Armonk! Makes great pepperoni!"

It stinks up the gym.

I look at Cockeye's face. His cross eyes make me uneasy. Which eye should I look into? His left or right? How embarrassing.

"Feel like sparring three rounds with Dino tomorrow?" I ask.

Cockeye eyes Dino. Then sits. The wooden bench groans. There's a lot of calories buried beneath Cockeye's underpants. "If he takes it easy."

"Great! See you at 4:00!" Honestly, sculpting beauty into Cockeye is hard. He's a fat, self-centered, lazy, aloof, grubby, mean-spirited, 25-year-old, but he's got a beautiful right hand.

The first chance I get, I throw the bloody chunks of meat into the dumpster behind the gym.

I'm desperate for sparring. I drive to the Mobil gas station on The Hutchinson Parkway to speak with Tiger, our pro. He says he'll box Dino, if he can get off work.

So, tomorrow is Dino's big test—he'll box Tiger, our alpha male, then Cockeye. Dino will need to focus. As the saying goes, *Nothing focuses the mind like one's own hanging.*

Wednesday, January 6:
Cockeye and Tiger are leaning on the red ring ropes waiting for me to fit on Dino's yellow headgear.

"Work with Cockeye for *power*," I whisper, greasing his face, "and Tiger for *speed*."

He inhales deep and lets it out real slow. I watch as he swivels his waist a few times, then steps through the ropes.

Dino does great. A small audience of boxers, Malcolm, Mayor Delphino and Andrew Spano, the Westchester County Executive, come to watch. The extra attention doesn't seem to distract Dino at all. He holds his own with Tiger. But there are still things to improve. For instance, Dino's face got a little busted up by Tiger's jab.

"My nose...," he says, softly. "...broke it."

I gently wiggle it. "Nah," I say, wiping him off, "you're not bleeding enough. Hey, this is gonna happen. Your nose'll get used to it."

Thursday, January 7:
Dino boxes six: two with Bobo; two with Cockeye, and the last two with Greg Zackar, the pro. Dino switches from defensive stylist, slipping punches, parrying and sidestepping, to aggressive stalker, slamming in double left hooks and uppercuts after lead rights. But Dino definitely needs more aggression. He needs to pivot with his left hook and sit down on punches, using his full foot for leverage. Flitting around the ring doesn't win amateur fights.

Tonight, Kid Corbett calls me at home. "If you need sparring, here's the phone number of Bobby Gleason's Gym—718-797-2872. Ask for Bruce Silverglade."

"Thanks, but you're still coming in with Zackar, right?"

"Nah. Zackar's too small."

"Zackar's a pro."

"Too small."

Is Dino scaring off pros?

Friday, January 8:

"Dino looks good!" beams Malcolm, poking his head into the gym. "We entering him into the Gloves? Since you work for me, I think I should know."

"Malcolm," I say, politely, "I work for the boys. Not you."

His face reddens and he walks away.

I think I'm right. Aren't I?

I guess I'll find out when I'm fired.

Monday, January 11:

Dino and I drive into Queens. We're taking our first official step towards The Golden Gloves Championship. In Dino's pocket is his *USA Boxing Registration Application* which he downloaded from the internet.

If you had told me 17 years ago that I'd be signing up a middleweight for The Golden Gloves, I'd have laughed. Even then I knew I needed to break away from this stupidity. But here I am, 17 years later, walking up the steps of Lost Battalion Hall on Queens Boulevard.

I'm crazy.

Is this my second shot at eighteen? Is this my comeback?

We walk in.

Monstrously muscled middleweights, angry lightheavys and seething heavyweights sit there quietly on metal chairs. It's eight long rows of silent human aberration. Each boy is wallowing within his own pungent anti-social delusion. Each kid is itching to explode.

Seeing them, there is an explosion of memory. Seventeen years ago, it was the same thick, regurgitated veneer of macho, the same tattoos, the same ugly faces, the same gold teeth, the same do-rags. I wondered then, as now, what family disasters, emotional perversions or mutated genes brought them here.

Sitting among them is my handsome olive-skinned, ex-junkie. I watch Dino sitting with this mob of miscreants and I have an odd thought: a baby rat has a better chance of running across Queens Boulevard before getting squished under a car tire, than a middleweight has of reaching the finals in Madison Square Garden.

It's a miserable 2 ½ hour wait just for Dino to get undressed, piss in a bottle, and be weighed. That's a long time when you don't dare socialize with the scuzzy sleazoid sitting on the metal chair next to you because you might be fighting him next week.

I pass time speaking with old Vic Zimet, a well-known New York City amateur trainer, who recognizes me from my fighting days.

"Peter Wood! How the hell are ya? Boy, I'll never forget how you knocked out my kid in the semifinals. Geesh! What a punch!"

It's nice to be remembered. "Your boy was kicking my butt before I finally caught him."

"He never fought again—Doctor's orders. And he was a good little fighter. Forget his name…"

"Walter Johnson," I say. His memory still breathes within me.

He nods. "He beat Harold Weston."

"Yeah?" Weston held the great Wilfred Benitez to a 10-round draw and later lost to him on a 15-round decision for the WBC Welterweight Championship. Not bad. Maybe I did miss *my calling* like Dom had said. I see myself, in green satin trunks, a shamrock on one leg and a Star of David on the other…But I quickly change channels. "Who you entering?" I ask.

Vic points to a skinny boy built like a thin #2 pencil. "He's Sephardic."

He doesn't look very impressive. His pink-rimmed eyes make him look like a white rat. "Good luck," I go.

Just then, Dino walks out, buttoning his shirt.

"What's your weight?" I ask.

"'Sixty-three."

"Geesh!" says Vic. "He looks like a heavyweight!"

"Skinny legs," I say.

Vic nods. "Like Emile Griffith."

Dino is flattered by the comparison. Emile Griffith is one of the greatest champions to emerge from the New York Golden Gloves—certainly the gayest champion.

I don't think Dino knew about the *gay* part.

A miracle!

Tonight, on my answering machine, is a message from a kid named Black Earl—I think that's what he said. He's a welterweight from Guyana. He has four amateur fights!

He's coming tomorrow!

We *need* sparring partners!

Guyana? Where is that? Africa? South America?

3

THE COOL DOWN

Boxing fascinates us because it appeals to the conservative, pent-up Republican in a three-piece suit who resides within us all.

—A. J. Liebling, The Sweet Science

Tuesday, January 12:

Black Earl, 19, is hopping up and down in the corner of the ring. He's tall and gangly and his shiny black skin is the color of a newly polished army boot. I've never seen skin on a kid so black and so tightly stretched. The muscle striations beneath his cheeks are painfully visible and his high cheekbones are virtually ripping out of his skin. His face is practically anorexic.

Dino's standing in the other corner. His chiseled abs and pecs glisten with a patina of sweat. Prancing up and down in the corner, he resembles a Roman god wearing boxing gloves. But a wise philosopher once said, *Any god who can be killed should be killed.*

I know I should be more cautious with Black Earl before putting him in the ring with Dino, but I'm desperate for sparring.

Clang!

Black Earl shuffles to the middle of the ring, feints, and lands a beautiful sucker-punch to Dino's left ear.

Dino stops dead. He shakes his left leg. "Cramp," he mutters.

"Come here," I say.

He *limps* over.

"I just told Earl to tear off your fucking head," I whisper. "Now, get going!" He needs to get used to harsh treatment if he's serious about winning The Gloves. But he keeps shaking his leg.

"Okay, step out," I mutter. "Maybe we're over-training. You taking salt?"

He stares ahead, sullenly.

Am I pushing him too hard? Perhaps we're not yet in synch and I'm over anxious. Maybe it's too early to correctly gauge his physical limits. I run my finger over his forehead and taste his sweat. Salty. Too salty.

I don't like how he's just standing there shaking his damn leg. I hope he isn't punking out. Every time he wusses out, *fear* grows stronger, and every time he doesn't, *he* grows stronger. It's a simple mathematical equation. Gym arithmetic.

Wednesday, January 13:

Dino didn't show.

Thursday, January 14:

Dino walks into the locker room and slumps to the locker room floor.

"Almost quit yesterday," he mutters.

I slide down beside him.

"Cried," he says. "Haven't cried since…my parents…"

Is he pulling a Tyson on me? As a 16-year-old amateur, Tyson was caught on tape whimpering before a fight.

"Last fight, I just stopped…hate that trait in myself," he whispers.

"What trait?"

Silence.

"What trait?" I repeat, softly.

"…I'm a quitter."

Silence.

"This tournament," I say, softly, "isn't about boxing. It's about Dino. Boxing introduces you to yourself."

He looks up. "I always wanted to get into a situation…where I could see how good I really am," he says.

I nod. "You're there."

"You think I can win?"

I smile big. "You're gonna crush these guys."

"You think?" His eyes go watery.

"It isn't how *I* see you, it's how *you* see you."

He looks down at his small hands.

"Dino, you said this was your dream. *Grab it.*"

Silence.

"Dino, look at me. People sometimes fear the very thing they want most."

He looks over my shoulder, somewhere into the past, and throws a few soft punches. "Thanks, Coach. My old trainer, never spoke like this…Not even my dad…He was a screamer, my Dad."

I feel like ruffling his black shiny hair, but don't. I admit it's endearing when he sits on the floor and looks at me like an 11-year-old boy, but he needs to grow up. Stop living in the residue of the past, Dino.

I'm beginning to really like this kid.

Wednesday, January 20:

We drive 15 miles south to Yonkers PAL. A Yonkers cop is waiting to spar. His square, cop face is rooted in anger. His ugly mug—pocked skin, whiskers, protruding cranial bone and slack-jaw, has so little beauty.

133

Clang!
Dino tears him apart.
"ONE MORE!" yells the cop.
They go one more and Dino dismembers him.

"That cop you just sparred was an open fighter and he couldn't touch you," I whisper, wiping sweat from Dino's untouched face.

Danny McAloon, a trainer, saunters over. "Your guy's gonna do well in The Gloves."

"He's gonna win it," I smile.

"I'd like him and my fighter, Joey Hughes, to spar, if you don't mind."

Hughes is the eighth-ranked amateur middleweight in America. He has national experience and has won inter-city tournaments in New York, Chicago and Detroit. He's perfect!

Thursday, January 21:

Tonight, Dino and I are driving to The Metro Boxing Championships, in Queens, for two critical reasons: to get the feel of a live boxing crowd, and to size up Joey Hughes.

In the car, I hand Dino a spaldine. "Squeeze it. Makes you punch harder."

Dino smiles. "Dad made me do this."

Two rows from ringside, we watch the bouts. At one point, a be-whiskered middle-aged man in the aisle is swinging punches, yelling encouragement.

Dino points. "See him?…He's like my dad." Dino stares at the man flailing his arms. "Between rounds, he always slapped my face."

Joey Hughes wins by second-round knockout. He hops down from the ring and we congratulate him. The skin on his tough Irish face, I notice,

has the rough surface of cowhide. Dino and Joey eyeball each other hard.
"See you in the gym," grins Joey, extending his bandaged hand.
Dino takes it and shakes.

Back in the car, I ask, "Can you handle Hughes?"
"He's ranked eighth," he says, tentatively.
"So?" I say. "All it takes is confidence."
He shrugs.

Friday, January 22:
"Confidence and courage!" I'm standing in front of the black-board with a stick of chalk in my hand. "Did Holden Caufield show confidence?...How about courage?..."
The class is grinning.
"So, who read?" I ask.
Now they're smirking.
"What's so funny?" I ask.
Shemika chuckles.
"So, no one read?"
Everyone laughs.
Great. In two years you stupid knuckleheads are gonna be:
a)   cleaning toilets.
b)   flipping burgers.
c)   collecting welfare.
d)   posing on porn websites.
e)   all of the above.

Shemika points to my 'Quote of the Day' written on the blackboard:

> *Life shrinks or expands in proportion to one's courage—*
> *Anais Nin.*

The class explodes with laughter. Some jerk has crossed out *courage* and has replaced it with *cojones. Balls.*

Just then I notice Sing-Sing standing in the doorway. She's dressed in a red dress and her long black hair is twisted in a loose-fitting bun, perched on the side of her head. She looks like a *Vanity Fair* clothing ad. The weak smile on her face doesn't quite cancel the disappointment of me I see in her eyes. "Sorry for interrupting your lesson, but this is for Jorge. It's his reminder for the after-school program." I feel a sudden knotting in my gut. *Sure I was once 34-1. But today I'm 0-1. Todd Rapier has knocked me out.*

Monday, January 25:

I walk into the locker room and find Dino sitting on the concrete floor. I hand him notice of his first bout. "February 3rd. Ten days."

He reads. "In Brooklyn."

"How you feel?"

"Wrist's...hurting," he says, swiveling it.

I tape it with extra gauze and adhesive tape. In order to protect his wrist, I fit on soft, 16-ounce, marshmallow gloves and concentrate on his right. I give him free shots to my belly. "Come on, punch hard!" I taunt.

I give him 35 free shots. "Weak! Weak! Weak...!" I shout. But, I don't give him a 36th.

At the end of the day, rubbing my sore stomach, I ask, "How's your wrist?"

"Sore."

"How you feel, otherwise?"

"If I stay healthy...I'll beat all those fighters," he says.

If? And I'm skeptical about his wrist. Am I seeing early signs of self-sabotage?

Wednesday, January 27:

Dino says his wrist feels fine, so we drive down to Yonkers PAL to spar.

Another cop is standing in the ring. He's a lanky Irishman with thick, bushy eyebrows and a dozen arm tattoos. Without his blue NYC Policeman's uniform, you'd swear he was a criminal.

"Keep your chin in, Dino," I caution.

Clang!

Dino dances for two rounds. He jabs and shows superb ring savvy. I'll be damned, he's almost elegant.

But after two, Dino looks wired. Something's wrong. His eyes are bulging.

"Relax," I say, kneading the back of his neck.

Clang!

The third round is pure artistry—until *something* happens. He starts wincing with each jab. At one point he grimaces and holds his left wrist.

"STOP!" I yell.

He walks back to the corner. "Glove's bothering me," he mumbles.

"Get out!" I snap. I escort him to the rear of the gym for privacy. "Let me tell you something. When I was in The Gloves, I created a lame excuse just before the finals—in case I lost. In short, I *did* lose. Now your first fucking fight's in nine days and you're already making excuses."

He stares blankly over my shoulder.

"Look at me! When people get stressed, they crack. In the finals, I cracked. I don't want that happening to you. Pressure is self-imposed. Don't let it cripple you."

Like it did me.

I phone him tonight at 7:00 at the house he's renting with a bunch of guys. "Hi, Dino, how's your wrist?"

"Better…but my thumb's hurting."

I'm speechless. Is he crazy? "Okay, come to the gym when you're ready." I hang up.I get no sleep tonight. I keep replaying Dino's third round in my mind. Now this bogus thumb excuse. What am I dealing with?

Floyd Patterson won the heavyweight title with a broken hand and Beau Jack fought a fight with a broken leg. Fact.

Thursday, January 28:

I have this gut feeling: boxing is not something Dino does because he enjoys it. He only does it because it relieves emotional pain, for a short time, anyway. Boxing is a sad happiness. I sense, for Dino, coming to the gym is a bit like going to the dentist for root-canal. He doesn't want to do it, but he feels better when it's over.

That afternoon, I find another sexy girl hiding in our locker room. She's swimming in the toilet bowl. I fish her out with a coat hanger. She's a dark-haired Spanish beauty, lying in bed, strapped up with leather restraints. Cockeye? Bobo? Tiger?

Friday, January 29:

Death walks into the gym. Dino. He's sickly pale and his black hair sticks out like crow feathers.

"You okay?" I ask.

He slumps to the floor and begins suiting up. "Not sleeping," he croaks.

"You're boxing Bobo and Black Earl. Can you handle that?"

He nods.

Bobo wallops him good and hard for two rounds. Black Earl beats him down for two.

Dino rips off his gloves with his teeth, dips out of the ring and stomps into the locker room.

It's horrible to see a kid self-destruct. It all started three days ago, when I told him the date of his first fight. First, it was his wrist, then his thumb, then he can't sleep and now he's getting beat up!

The jerk's sitting on the concrete room floor, pouting. He tosses his handwraps into his dufflebag.

"What's the matter?"

He kicks off his shoes.

"You're fighting in seven days," I remind him.

"Don't know who's gonna show up." He shrugs his muscular shoulders. "…I'll just go and see."

"That's not good enough!" I spit. "You'll train hard for seven days and win."

"...I'll *try*," he says, half-heartedly.

"*Try?*" I explode. "There ain't no *trying* to it! *Trying* is when you were five-years-old and got credit for tying your shoelace! You either do it or don't!"

Monday, February 1:

Dino walks in. I follow him into the locker room. He slumps to the floor.

"What's wrong?" I ask.

"Me?...Nothing...Why?" It's as if he didn't know what I'm talking about. It's like a thin piece of emotional Plexiglas is separating us.

"I gotta get...cocky," he says, pulling off his black sock. "Never been cocky."

"Cocky?" I say, shaking my head. "Quiet confidence, Dino, is what you want."

He looks up at me.

I squat down to his level. "You definitely don't want *cocky*. Confidence is a balancing act. Too much, you're cocky; too little, you're unconfident—both cripple you."

He pulls off his other black sock and thinks about it.

"Let's not think too much, okay?" I say. "Let's just take it one step at a time."

"Like a 12-step program?"

"Yeah," I grin. "Now get ready to spar.

In the ring, Dino comes alive. He's double jabbing and hooking and feinting and uppercutting. He could have knocked Bobo out at any point. Dino's back on track.

I realize, while swabbing blood out of his nose with a Q-tip, that I really like this strange, sullen kid.

Later, I left him alone to hit the bags. Maybe I hover over him too much.

Tuesday, February 2:

We pull into the Yonkers PAL parking lot. Dino is scheduled to spar Ugly Cop.

But he's not there.

The only boxer in the gym is Joey Hughes.

I approach his trainer. "Our fight's in three days. My guy needs work. He'll go three two-minute rounds with Joey..."

"...if Joey goes easy, right?" he chuckles.

Clang!

Dino promptly hands Joey Hughes, the eighth-ranked amateur middleweight in America, a boxing lesson! Dino catches him repeatedly with sneaky right hands and snappy left hooks. Dino's bopping Joey's nose with a variety of punches; never throwing the same combo twice in succession. If it were a sanctioned bout, Dino would've won.

"Brilliant!" I whisper, as Dino steps out of the ring. "You took him to school!"

He flashes a champion's smile.

I don't tell him that Joey went easy on him.

Wednesday, February 3:

Tiger, wearing his brown Mobil uniform, peddles into the gym on his red Schwinn. "She ain't pretty, but I put her together myself."

"Tiger," I say, "I'll pay you $10 a round to spar Dino."

"Good God, Coach! I'll do it for nothing!"

"I know, but I need sparring and your skills are worth it," I say.

"Oh, Coach!" he says, draping his long muscular arms around me.

I like Tiger. He's got a certain simian grace. When he fights, his punches are like guttural utterances like *Smash, Boss, Eat, Cash.* I think boxing is his outlet to express himself, and to let the world know he isn't just some cockroach even if he does wear a brown uniform.

Thursday, February 4:

It's the day before Dino's first fight and I want him in the gym just to break a sweat and discuss strategy for a southpaw.

While Dino and I shadowbox in the ring, a woman reporter from *The Journal News* snaps photos. Suddenly, Dino bounces a looping right onto my jaw. I feel nothing but, for effect, I drop to a knee, then crumble to the canvas.

Dino gasps.

"Wha happen?" I slur, blinking my eyes.

Dino lifts me up.

"Goo shot," I mumble, rubbing my jaw. "Do that fight night." I look over at the horrified photographer. "You didn't snap that, did ya?"

4

THE FIRST PRELIMINARY

I now find the whole subject of professional boxing disgusting. Except for the fighters, you're talking about human scum, nothing more. Professional boxing is utterly immoral. It's not capable of reformation. You'll never clean it up. Mud can never be clean.

—Howard Cosell

Friday, February 5:

Fight night. Brooklyn.

Dino's old neighborhood.

Dino's fight-plan: *1) Whatever you do, do it fast.*

2) When in doubt—jab.

3) Dip low before you throw your left hook.

Three basic principles are enough for any nervous kid to remember.

We're driving down Atlantic Avenue. Dino points to an Army recruitment center. "Enlisted there."

"What made you join?"

"Dad was army."

"Oh?"

"Worst thing…rappelling drills."

"Why?"

"Heights scare me."

"That's why didn't you stay in?"

"No…broke my foot…Bad things always happen."

Heights scare me?…Bad things always happen?

In the parking lot, we grab our gear and lock the car.

We spot two shadowy figures, carrying dufflebags, walking down into a parish hall basement: Dom Bufano and Tony Malzone, the garbage-eater.

"Put your game face on," I instruct. *"Don't look at anyone—everyone looks at you. The time to win a fight is before it actually starts. You hit a fighter in the brain before you actually hit him on the head."* Dom taught me well.

Dino nods.

In the basement, boxers are already stripping down for their physicals. It's funny. All these vicious thugs will soon be killing off billions of each other's brain cells, but now they're all modestly stripped down to *two* sets of underwear—usually a silky Speedo beneath a jockey bikini. Spanish guys, I note, are wearing the more colorful bikinis. Dino is wearing two pairs of underwear, too. Orange paisley and green stripe.

As far as physiques go, Dino is chiseled. His body fat is freakishly low and his torso looks like it's been swabbed with posing oil and competition coloring. A physique doesn't make him a champ, but just looking at Dino could give a guy the willies and make him want to go home and crawl back into bed. But I fear Dino might be a bit like the 1934 Heavyweight Champion, Max Baer, *the man with the million-dollar body and the ten-cent brain.* Baer's tenure as world title-holder lasted only one year—1934.

"All fighters, weigh in!" shouts a horn-like voice.

"Remember," I whisper, wanting to keep his potent left hand secret, "sign in with your *right*."

Dom Bufano finds a quiet spot for his protégé in the corner. Then he ambles over to us and extends his hand to Dino. "Good luck, son." Now I feel obligated to wish Tony the same—it probably has something to do with my mother's preoccupation with formality and etiquette.

I walk over. Tony's slouched in a wooden seat, bragging how he's "going to crack" his opponent's skull. He looks confident. But I swear, I smell fear radiating off his sweaty white back. You fraud. "Good luck," I grin.

I walk back to Dino. Camped next to us is a batch of pent-up Puerto Ricans. They're doing a lousy job of camouflaging their nerves with noisy chatter and laughter. They bother me. I wanna smack each one on the head.

We sit down and wait. The most miserable part of boxing is the wait. Ask any fighter. You throb through each second. That's just how it is.

Dino, stonefaced, drapes a white towel over his head and listens to his Walkman. A lot of fighters are plugged into Walkmans—an invention of isolation and comfort.

A stooped-shouldered troll walks up to me. His bent-nosed middleweight, a guy with tartar-stained teeth and a lot of pent-up hostility, stands behind him. The troll points to my silver necklace with two silver gloves embracing a bright ruby. "Are those the Golden Gloves?"

I nod. My Golden Gloves necklace is my badge of identity. Very few boxers win them. It proves I'm exceptional. I cling to it pitifully. I know it's pathetic to need a necklace to make me feel good, but without it, I'm just a soft overweight English teacher sitting in some Brooklyn parish hall basement.

"Hey, Gary," says the troll, turning to his fighter, "those're the gloves you're gonna win."

The troll begins asking me more questions, but hey, I'm not his damn friend. He quickly interprets my unfriendly expression and moves on.

The referees, dressed in starched white uniforms, march into the basement. They stand on chairs and bark their instructions like Nazis. I listen to these tough NYC trainers ass-kiss them with questions. Maybe they're just being politically smart. Boxing is not without its politics.

Dino is the fourth bout. Not bad—there are twenty. We drew an unattached guy with no gym affiliation—that's excellent.

"Where's he at?" murmurs Dino.

"Don't know," I say, taping his hands with two rolls of gauze and the maximum amount of tape—two yards. I hold his hands in order for my warmth, strength and confidence to ooze into his fingers.

I soon discover our opponent...Gary, the troll's kid!

Dino steps into his new purple-satin trunks. I think they're ugly, too long in the leg, but if he's happy, I'm happy. My thin worn, yellow headgear is stashed in my dufflebag—it's not the authorized headgear officials insist boxers wear. In my opinion, their chubby helmet makes a boxer get hit even more and gives him brain damage.

"Dino Lazaro and Gary Paine! Get your gloves!" yells a voice. A pair of canary yellow gloves and additional adhesive tape is handed to us. Quietly, I strap on our thin personal headgear. With luck, we'll sneak by.

I hold up my right palm. "Throw your over-hand right."

BOOM!

"Straight right."

BOOM!

"Right uppercut."

BOOM!

It's three tires exploding. I'm not kidding.

"Now surprise him with your *left*," I whisper.

Dino sits. I crouch between his legs and put my hands on his knees. "This is how it'll be in the corner. I talk—you listen. But when the bell rings, it's just you and him—no me, no crowd, no nothing. Understand?"

He nods.

9:30—A Golden Gloves usher with a gray mustache camouflaging his cleft-palette, calls us upstairs. He peers into Dino's eyes and whispers, "You got *the look*. I'm a wizard-genius at these things. You're gonna win."

Wish I could agree. Dino's sad wet eyes are glassy with fear. His neck vein pulses.

Our wizard-genius escorts us onto an old wooden stage with purple velour curtains. Behind the curtains, the crowd roars. Dino's opponent, Gary Paine, is loosening up beside us.

Dino kneels in a corner and prays. Who is he praying to? God? His father? His mother?

"LAZARO—BLUE CORNER!...PAINE—RED CORNER!"

We walk down the aisle to the ring and Dino hops in.

I look across the ring. Paine is already inside, pacing like a tiger, throwing short ominous hooks. He's ready to eviscerate my boy.

"This guy's gonna rush you," I predict.

Dino looks scared.

Clang!

5

THE WRITE UP

When I got in the ring for my first fight I listened to the crowd. It was the first time in my life I ever heard people cheering for me.

—Vito Antuofermo, middleweight champion

...I'm right. Paine charges, winging wild, nervous punches. Dino crouches low and springs up with a left hook that nails him flush. Paine reels back. Dino clobbers him again with an over-hand right and a sweeping left hook. Paine drops. Coolly, Dino walks to a neutral corner and looks down at me.

Clang!

"Great!" I say. "Watch him switching lefty." It's a hunch. Someone once said *the irrational is not necessarily unreasonable.* Paine is so outclassed he'll need to go into emergency mode and do *some*thing, *anything*—even if it's crazy. He'll need to throw himself on anything that resembles hope. I didn't want Dino to be nailed by a far-fetched gimmick or by a *Hail Mary.* "Just find an angle, dip, and throw your left-hook."

"Did I win that round?" says Dino, breathing heavily.

"Yeah, you won! You knocked him down! Now win this round!" *Clang!*

In the middle of the round, Dino grows more confident and moves in cautiously. Suddenly, he finds his opening and attacks. He starts beating the hell out of Paine's face, burying lefts and rights into his nose. In desperation, Paine turns his back and runs. He looks like a swimmer escaping from a wave before it smashes upon him. Dino chases, grabs Paine's shoulder and spins him. He's about to shatter his front teeth when the referee stops it.

I bound into the ring. "Great job!" I tear off his headgear. I want the crowd to connect with my boy and shower him with love. "Congratulate Paine and bow to the audience."

People are cheering.

Reporters from *The New York Times,* the *Daily News* and *The Reporter Dispatch* are interviewing him and snapping pictures. It's great to be a winning fighter. Even soreness feels fine.

Back in the basement, some Puerto Rican trainer is shaking Dino's hand. "*Tu eres el campeon,*" he whispers. Dino smiles.

"Dino, don't smile," I caution. "Let them wonder about you. Let them get nervous." (Another Dom Bufano ploy.)

"*Muy fuerte, chico…,*" continues the trainer.

"Talk English," I bark.

He didn't like that, but that was just too damn bad. "Why?" he spits. "There be more Spanish-speaking people in this world than English."

"*Quando habla con me peleador,*" I say, remembering a few snatches of college Spanish, "*y yo estoy aqui, habla English.*" If you want to speak to my fighter when I'm around, speak English.

He steps back and hisses. But he left, that's all I care about. Don't need a schizoid freak playing the race-card to steal my fighter.

Dino receives $10 carfare and gets to keep his blue Golden Gloves tee shirt.

"Get dressed, dry your hair, and we'll go up and scout our competition," I say.

We enter the crowd and a batch of spectators cluster around Dino; one young boy asks for his autograph.

"Sign righty," I whisper. A fan, in his thirties with surplus body flesh, buys Dino a Coke. Other spectators pat Dino's muscular back.

Winning a fight is great—it puts you in a warm fog where people kiss your ass, tell you that you're wonderful and allows you to begin to think you're a great guy. But deep down the fans hate your guts. They hate you because they are fat or lazy or because they are disgusted with themselves for eating that second hotdog. They hate you because they can't defer gratification or because they can't sublimate their fears or because they hate you because they just hate you. It's simple—they just want you down on their level.

Unfortunately, we missed Tony Malzone's bout. He knocked out a tough PAL fighter in the first. "He looked like a white Sugar Ray Robinson," beams Dom.

Yeah, right, Dom. *The best liar wins.*

Sitting quietly in the audience, scouting us, is Joey Hughes. It's a bit like being stalked, but that's okay. We stalked *him.*

Dino drove home with a friend, (actually, a friend of a friend.) He was the only *friend* Dino had in the audience.

Before going to bed, I telephone Dino. "I just wanted to know you got back safe."

"Thanks."

"I'm proud of you. You were beautiful tonight."

"Thanks."

"That was nice, your friend coming."

"Yeah, well…"

I smell the sadness in his voice. "You're the next champ, Dino."

"Thanks, Coach."

Hanging up the phone, I understand his sadness. Only one

person bought a ticket to watch him fight his heart out. Where is his foster family? His roommates? His friends? A girlfriend?

This poor kid is utterly alone.

Saturday, February 6:
I wake up early to buy the *Daily News*. I read:

Lazaro Lights It Up

*First bout jitters are difficult to keep
under control and nobody had a more
difficult time than Gary Paine. He came
out of his corner like a wildman and
was all over the place. Dino Lazaro of
White Plains found a way to slow
Paine down. A short right hand from
Lazaro caught Paine on the chops and
dropped him. Paine was more cautious
in round two, but Lazaro didn't care,
and with a series of combinations,
Paine was done and the 165-pound bout
was stopped. 'I figured any opponent
would come out wild, and he did,' said
Lazaro. 'I calmed myself down and
just waited for him.' Lazaro's ability
to stay under control not only won him
the bout, but the 'NobodyBeats the Wiz
Boxer of the Night' honors, as well.*

"Did I win that round?" He's so fucking unaware of himself.

Dino's blooming.

6

ANOTHER SELF DESTRUCTIVE PUNK

You're not in condition, you're gonna get your
brains scattered to the wrong part of your head.
Can't never quit in a ring. All that crap about
defense—take it and put it up your butt.
Conditioning.

—Beau Jack, lightweight champ in the 1940s

Tuesday, February 9:

Dino's next bout is February 25th. Sixteen days.

Today he boxes three platonic rounds with Tiger. Platonic is okay the first day back, but watching Tiger encouraging Dino while sparring him is too patronizing. *Damnit! Go after him, Dino!*

Tiger—tall, rangy and quick—is perfect for Dino. He's sneaky in a cute way, much like Pernell "Sweetpea" Whitaker, the great lightweight and welterweight champ of the 1990s. Tiger throws his long arm out, and if you flinch, he probably won't throw a punch. But if you don't, Tiger'll pop you. Dino must be on his toes.

Wednesday, February 10:

I knead Dino's neck as he looks over at Black Earl in the opposite corner. "This time, box two nice rounds," I whisper, "then go after him in the third."

Clang!

For two rounds, Black Earl's bean-pole jab spears Dino's face. Dino is sort of, kind of, vaguely, fighting back. What's wrong, Dino? What is it about Black Earl you can't handle? You scared of black fighters? Earl's black as coal.

They never reach the second round—Dino walks out.

Black Earl has been training with us for the past month. Like Tyrone and Stuttering Bobo, he favors ghetto chic—spindly braids, gangsta-clothing and droopy pants. Black Earl, I've learned, is a minister's son. Back in Guyana, he was an honor student. Although he's tall and smart, he thinks he's small and stupid. He's always slouching and sucking his crooked yellow teeth. Something dark seems to be pulling at his Earl's heart.

Two years ago, Black Earl and his friend were caught robbing a man at the White Plains train depot. Their weapon was a long black snake. Newspapers said Earl's accomplice held the man while Black Earl shoved a hissing snake into the victim's face.

Wonder what type of snake.

Thursday, February 11:

Tonight, I drive to Bed Stuy to scout seven middleweight bouts—I'm eager to study our competition. I arrive early and have a half-hour before the matches start, so I walk around in the frigid cold looking for a bookstore. It's so cold, my nose hair freezes. I remember as a young boy, before I had any fights, I'd sleep on my nose to bend it in order to look more like a fighter. Now, after 35 fights, I'm a noisy-nose breather and my nostrils whistle and drag with mucous.

Walking down this rundown Brooklyn street, I'm remembering Tyrone Crooks—this was his neighborhood. Strewn trash, shattered glass, crumbling warehouses tagged with gang graffiti. I will not find a bookstore here.

I hop into a *bodega* and buy a *Sports Illustrated*. There's an article about Aaron Pryor, the former 1980-85 welterweight champion who became a crack-addict. Now he shadowboxes on Cincinnati street corners for coins. Great sport, boxing.

I scout 14 middleweights. Of the seven winners, five can beat Dino.

Especially a black kid named Sidney Nahiem from Bed-Stuy. But I'm glade I went tonight because I now know for sure who Dino's next opponant is. I'm dead safe

Friday, February 12:

Dino walks into the gym office looking miserable. "My dad died today."

"I'm sorry." I pat his shoulder. He winces.

"Shoulder's hurting," he says, rotating it.

I'm not liking this one damn bit. "Take the day off," I say.

"Nah…it's okay."

Dino, don't get weak on me.

We drive down to Yonkers. Black Earl comes.

This time, it's reversed—Joey Hughes takes Dino to school. It isn't pretty, but tough sparring is what Dino needs.

After three brisk rounds, I towel Dino off. "Let me remind you, Joey's an *open* fighter. He's nationally ranked and you aren't. You are who you fight."

He looks at me weird.

Simone de Beauvoir once said something similar: *You are who you fuck.* She was talking about women who seek men to bed because it gives them sexual valuation.

Similarly, Roberto Duran's sparring partner, Alex Quiroga, a 24-year-old welterweight from Miami, was taking a beating in the gym one day. After Quiroga sustained a black eye, he handed Duran a felt-tipped pen and asked him to autograph his face.

Strange world, boxing.

Driving back to White Plains, I point to Black Earl quietly sucking his yellow teeth in the back seat. "Dino, see Earl? He's on three-year probation for robbery."

"You, too?" says Dino.

My eyes dart in Dino's direction.

"I once broke a kid's arm...Street fight," says Dino. "Over a girl...Slammed a car door him. Kept slamming...Aggravated assault."

"How old were you?" asks Black Earl, sucking his crooked yellow teeth.

"Seventeen."

"Any other problems?" I ask.

"Once broke a kid's jaw."

"Why?"

"Harassing my friend."

"Boxing makes ugly energy beautiful," I say, hoping it was true.

I glance at Black Earl in the rear-view mirror. "By the way, what kind of snake was it?"

He shrugs. "I dunno. Some big black sucker."

Monday, February 15:

Today Dino is scheduled to box in Yonkers, but he never shows. No call, no nothing.

I call. No answer. I call again. No nothing.

His fight is in ten days!

His shoulder? Is he going psychosomatic?

Wednesday, February 17:

Still no Dino.

It's been two days.

At 4:30, I call.

"He's in bed," says a roommate.

"Wake him up."

Dino answers, groggily. "I'm sick."

"What's wrong?"

"Vomiting."

You're bullshitting me, aren't you, you prick? "Okay, sigh, don't train this weekend. Relax. Call me Monday."

"Okay."

"Dino…"

"What?"

"I know who your next opponant is."

"huh?

"Time's running out Dino."

"You only have eight days left."

"Who am i fighting"

"Can you do it?"

"Uh-huh."

"Are you…head-banging?" I almost ask. But how can I ask such a thing?

I'm depressed. I'm discovering that Dino might not have the emotional stamina to hang in. He might be the type of kid who cracks under pressure, or collapses under the strain of day-to-day contact with others, or bursts with the thought of losing, or crumbles with the possibility of winning, or unravels at the thought that he's unworthy, or disintegrates at the burden of his past, or cowers anticipating the future. He might be the type of kid endowed with all the physical gifts, but who ends up shooting himself in the head.

Friday, February 19:

Malcolm pops his head into the gym. "How's our Dino doing?'

I throw him a dirty look.

"Should we be laying down bets?"

I grin and give him a thumbs up. Go to hell.

Sunday, February 21:

Dino's fight is in four days and for the last five he's been lying in bed. A young fighter needs three to four rounds of sparring a day, at least; plus six to ten rounds on the bags and three miles of roadwork. Somewhere, some angry New York City punk has been, every day, lacing on a pair of 16-ounce Everlast boxing gloves preparing to kick Dino's butt.

At 7:30, I call him.

"Hi," he croaks. "I'm laying flat on my back."

Tyrone Crooks' face flashes through my mind—he's lying on a prison cot with a shitter two inches from his nose. I see myself 17 years ago lying flat on the gym canvas pretending to be knocked out by a light heavyweight. Sometimes, the most comfortable thing to do *is* lie down. But not now!

"Do you still want to fight?" I ask, softly.

"Uh-huh," he coughs.

You sure?"

"Uh-huh."

"You got enough oranges?"

"Uh-huh who am I fighting?"

"You taking vitamins?"

"Uh-huh coach, who am I fighting?"

"Shut up and listen. I have an assignment for you. Get a pencil..."

"Don't got one."

"Go get one!" I suddenly shout. "And a piece of paper!"

"Okay, okay..." he croaks. He's gone a long minute.

"Now draw a big circle," I instruct.

"A circle?"

"Yes. A big fucking circle! Do it!"

"Uh-huh."

"In the middle of the circle, write your goal."

"Goal?"

"Yes! Your fucking goal! Are you listening, or what?"

"Listenin'."

"Write your fucking goal inside. If it's to win this year's Golden Gloves, write that. Okay?"

"Uh-huh."

"Underline it."

"Uh-huh."

"Then, inside the circle, write all the reasons *why* you desire this goal."

"Uh-huh."

"Then, outside the circle, write all the obstacles stopping you from achieving this goal."

"Uh-huh."

"Then tape it to your fucking mirror."

"Uh-huh."

"Dino, are you throwing away your ability, or striving for your dream?"

"Strive...," he coughs.

"For my *dream!* Say it!"

"...dream."

"Then, do it! And when you're finished, bring that fucking paper in, I want to see it."

"Uh-huh...coach, who..."

I slam down the phone, my heart's racing. I don't know why I'm yelling, but next to Crooks, Dino might be the most insane, self-destructive punk I've ever met. *Who is his next opponent? It's obvious.*

Dino's fighting Dino.

7

THE SECOND
PRELIMINARY

I was always right on the edge of the top echelon.
The edge seemed to be my destiny.

—Wilfy Greaves, middleweight contender

Tuesday, February 23:

Dino drags himself into the gym and slumps to the floor. It's been seven days! *When the Music's Over* by The Doors is playing in the background.

"Where's that sheet of paper?" I ask. "With the circle on it?"

He shrugs.

"You got it?"

He shakes his head.

"Why not?"

"No pencil," he says, staring blankly.

You sonofabitch! You're a Tyrone Crooks!

"Coach, I can only train three days a week...Work-schedule's changing."

I throw up my arms. "Dino, you want the title, or not?"

"Job's important, Coach."

"So's the title."

"Boss needs me."

"Dino, first it's your wrist, then it's your thumb, then you're sick, then you're sick again, then it's your shoulder, then, today you look like shit, and now it's your boss—when's it gonna fucking end?" It's sickening.

...when the music's over...

"When's this schedule-change occurring?" I ask.

"March 30th."

"We'll worry about it then," I say. I look at his sad face. This is one of the most significant events in the history of his miserable life. It's serious stuff, like the Olympics, and this poor, fragile kid is scared shitless. This is when a boy needs his mother.

"Here," I say. "I brought you something." I haul out my boxing scrapbook. I point to a scowling face in the Golden Gloves Finals fight program. "That's me. I look more Puerto Rican than you do."

His face registers no response.

I point to James Hargroves, my stable-mate. "Look at this beast. I sparred this guy five days a week. He was my Joey Hughes. Eventually, I got to where I could beat him. The same with you. But you got to *work* at it."

No response.

I point to other mugshots. "Here's Vito Antuofermo, the World Middleweight Champ...Here's Eddie Gregory, the Light Heavyweight Champ...Here's Leroy Jones, he fought Larry Holmes for the Heavyweight Championship. And guess what? Your face belong here. too."

I look at his blank stare. I don't think I'm getting through. He's comatose.

...when the music's over...

Tonight an official calls from The Golden Gloves and cancels Dino's

February 25ᵗʰ fight! Scheduling problem! Dino's next fight is March 11ᵗʰ! *Divine Intervention!*

Wednesday, February 24:

When Dino shuffles in, I tell him he lucked out. He looks relieved, but still blighted.

"Stomach hurts," he groans.

I've had it. I'm sick of him. He's too high-maintenance. I'm killing this punk with attention, and what for? An ulcer? I let Bobo suit him up.

Dino spars three pathetic rounds with Tiger—he's just going through the motions. I watch silently as he continually steps inside, refuses to punch, and holds. It's the ready-aim-aim-aim-syndrome. PUNCH! DAMN YOU!

At the end of his workout, I say, "Okay, let me weigh you. You said you had weight problems. Step on the scale."

He hits 163 pounds exactly.

Bullshit, he's fine.

"You looked shitty today," I say. "I'll tell you when you look good and I'll tell you when you look shitty."

"Couldn't punch…Tiger tied me up."

"Don't hand me that! You just didn't punch. You have a problem with blacks? You scared of blacks?"

"No," He mumbles.

"Then let's get with it, man!" I point to March 11th on the calendar. "If you don't pick up by then, I'm scratching you, and I don't mean maybe. You're gonna feel like a horse's ass getting knocked out."

"Ain't getting knocked out."

"Yes you are! Out of the tournament! By me!"

Thursday, February 25:

Dino knocks Stuttering Bobo's mouthpiece out of the ring in the second. That flying mouthpiece, flipping over the top ring-rope, does wonders for Dino's confidence.

Mine, too.

Black Earl steps in next. Dino moves a bit better with him, but after one round, Dino's winded. Is he doing roadwork? I doubt it.

But my faith is somewhat restored by Bobo's airborne mouthpiece. And he did box better against Black Earl—even if it was for only one round.

Bedding the gym down for the night, I find another naked girl hiding in the locker room. She's a pretty blonde with a shotgun between her long, thin legs. She's crumpled up beneath a locker. Who's doing this? Tiger, Cockeye or Stuttering Bobo. Must be.

Friday, February 26:

Dino shuffles in.

"How you doing?" I ask.

"Got a fever," he croaks.

Damn! I can't even ask this guy how he's doing without a sob story! "Well," I say, softly, "go home."

"It's okay," he says.

"Look, after one round, if you look terrible, you're out."

Dino steps into the ring with Tiger and boxes like a champ. Even Tiger congratulates him. Guess Dino forgot he was sick.

Next, he batters the heavybag. His sweat drops splattering the floor are now the size of nickels—there must be $2 worth. My confidence in him is yo-yoing. Maybe I should distance myself. Maybe he feels more comfortable alone. Some people feel more comfortable alone.

It's Friday—6:00. I drive home, eat, and go to bed. Yeah, some people feel more comfortable alone. Like me. But I miss Sing-Sing.

Tuesday, March 9:

Where's my hypochondriac?

My knotting stomach is becoming ulcerous. Dino hasn't trained in seven days. Today is crucial—it's his last day sparring. He's only sparred five rounds for this fight—I did that in one day! I call his house but no answer. I'm sick and tired of this little weasel.

When I get home at 7:00, there's a message on my answering machine: "*Cough-cough...*sick as a dog...*cough*...see ya tomorrow."

Wednesday, March 10:

Dino never shows. I can't believe this bum. He fights tomorrow! He's not ready! I phone his home and his roommate answers. "What's wrong with Dino?"

"Don't ask me, ask him. He's lying in bed."

Dino picks up. "Can't get food down...puking," he coughs.

"Try some soup, chicken barley."

"Can't...religious holiday."

Oh? That's a new one. What observance is that? Saint Psychosomatic Day? "Okay, vegetable soup and dry toast. Eat something."

"Coach, I got something important to say..."

Oh, no, here it comes...

"Remember when I first met you? I lied...Never had one hundred fights."

"It's okay, Dino."

He mumbles something I can't make out.

"Look," I say, "if you feel like showing up tomorrow, great. If not, that's fine, too. It's all good."

"I'll be there," he whispers.

This poor guy's spiralling down fast. He's fighting tomorrow, he's a huge favorite, and he's lying flat on his back, puking. Maybe a championship is too much to ask. When the chips are down, in some guys—as fixed in them as their bone structure—is a deep, rich, dark pessimism, an unquenchable subconscious attachment to self-destruction.

If he shows up tomorrow, I'll weigh him. If his weight is low, I'll appeal to the officials for a bye and try to keep him afloat for as long as possible.

This evening, while eating a chicken parm wedge, pickle and coleslaw at my kitchen table I remember the "Five Rules of the World" as arrived at by one of my Jesuit professors at Fordham. *The first rule: You must not have anything wrong with you or anything different. The second rule: If you do have something wrong with you, you must get over it as soon as possible. The third rule: If you can't get over it, you must pretend that you have. The fourth rule: If you can't even pretend that you have, you shouldn't show up. You should stay home, because it's hard for everyone else to have you around. And the fifth rule: If you are going to insist on showing up, you should at least have the decency to feel guilt and shame.*

Thursday, March 11:

Fight night.

Dino walks in. He doesn't look guilty or shameful. He's calm and relaxed.

"Dino, I feel like smacking the shit out of you," is what I should say. Instead, I say, "Feeling okay?"

He nods.

Is this the eye of the storm?

I point to the scale. "Step on."

He hits 162 pounds. Perfect!

We hop into the car at 5:30 and drive to Glen Cove High School in Long Island. It's a miserable hour-and-fifteen-minute drive with traffic.

"Is your friend coming tonight?" I ask, making small talk.

He shrugs.

Unfortunately, we drew Sidney Nahiem. "Probably Jewish," I say, trying to buoy his spirits with the prospects of an easy win.

"Or Muslim," Dino responds, sullenly.

Unfortunately, Nahiem *is* Black Muslim, and he fights out of a tough club—NYC PAL. Nahiem is the wiry black kid with excellent hand speed, and a knockout punch, who I was worried about.

I'm watching Nahiem warming up in the shower area; his muscular shoulders and rippling abs are glisting with sweat. His hair is braided in cornrows and he's chewing a toothpick. Various tribal trinkets are slung around his thick neck. But the most disturbing aspect about him is that he's the spitting image of Black Earl—black as pitch. I glance at Dino's face and see a sick, weak-kneed expression.

Maybe I'm projecting.

Fifteen minutes before their match, Nahiem and Dino stand side by side getting fit for gloves. Suddenly, Nahiem's trainer throws his arms up in disgust. "You forgot *what?*"

"My mouthpiece," whispers Nahiem.

"You crazy fool! Now you gotta use Izzy's!" blurts his trainer.

Two minutes later, his trainer scoffs, "You stupid, stupid jerk! I can't believe you!" Nahiem is holding his protective-cup; he forgot to put it on beneath his trunks! His poor humiliated heart must be howling. His trainer shouldn't be berating him like that directly in front of his opponent. It's shameful. It's terrible when a boxer is emotionally unprepared —especially if you're that boxer.

"He's scared to death," I whisper, just in case Dino missed it.

Dino's lucky Nahiem's in such bad shape, and doubly lucky Nahiem doesn't know how fragile and unprepared he is.

Clang!

Nahiem rushes and burrows his cornbraided hair into Dino's sweaty armpit; I guess he figures it's the safest place. Nahiem wrestles and muscles Dino around the ring without throwing much leather.

It quickly develops into a non-fight fight, a wrestling match of grab, hold and push. I guess it's Nahiem's plan—to survive. But it looks like Nahiem's the aggressor because Dino is being thwarted and shoved around and doesn't get anything off. Honestly, it doesn't look like Dino's trying all that hard.

I'm sick to my gut with frustration. The elite fighter I've trained in the gym and the guy floating around in the ring aren't the same guys. Dino's drifting in some half-dreamt fugue state. What Dino is doing is choreography, not boxing. He's posing and being passively cute.

Suddenly, the mustachioed man at The Metros, *Dino's father*, hollers inside my brain. *Slap Dino.*

No way.

I look up into the ring. Dino is just pitty-pattying and flitting around. He's like a thin, flat rock thrown on water skimming the surface without taking the plunge.

Clang!

"Get angry!" I shout into his face.

He sits and stares blankly.

"This ain't no I.Q. test! Start rumbling!" I grab his head and splash water in his face. I want to slap him.

The second round is worse. He flounders around, chicken-pecking his jab. It's mild violence. Yeah, Dino looks cute, but he's losing.

Between rounds, I again fight the urge to slap his lousy face. He's doing nothing!

In the third, Nahiem is finally penalized one point for holding and rabbit punching. It's an ugly, messy affair and Dino can't—or *won't*—display his talent or show off his arsenal of punches. They're clinching and clutching and so tangled up in each other's arms it verges on intercourse.

Clang!

Dino walks back to the corner. I look at the dead wall of his sweaty face. With a disturbing mixture of detachment and nonchalance, he shrugs. "I lost."

"It's close," I admit, "but you won."

The vote is close—2-1. We squeaked by.

Back in the dressing room, Dino walks out of the toilet stall wiping his mouth with the back of his taped hand. "Just puked," he mutters.

I look in the stall. Inside, a bloodied heavyweight, too dainty to touch the metal handle with his hand, is gingerly flushing the toilet with the toe of his white-tasseled boxing shoe.

There's spittle and splatter and urine everywhere, but no vomit.

When I return, Dino is in the throes of a sneezing fit—a full two minutes of violent sneezing. I've never seen anything like it. It's the most impressive thing Dino has done all night. A two-minute seizure. I'm not kidding. He's lucky he didn't sneeze up an adenoid. I almost call the doctor. Is this an allergic reaction? But to what? Success?

Something painful is squirming inside this kid and I can't put my finger on it. I want this tournament to be a meaningful experience, but he never cracks a smile. I never know what's behind the barrier of his heart, or the wall of his face. Who's in there? I don't even know if he likes me. I'm not supposed to care about things like that because, well, I'm the coach and the coach isn't supposed to get soft about those things. But it's been two months now and except for knowing that he was a heroin addict, hates heights, broke his foot in the army, and bad things always happen to him, I'm no closer to understanding him.

Maybe it's my fault. Perhaps *I'm* deficient.

But Dino doesn't let you get close. I bet even his roommates are strangers. Most good boxers I've known tend to distrust others and are alienated from the people around them. That's the true boxing spirit—independence. If I want a champion, then I must encourage him to be independent, even from me. But he's so damn distant already. There are times when he does talk. Most of the time, though, he has the personality of a mannequin.

Tony Malzone, Dom's garbage-eating protégé, scores another brilliant first-round knockout. Clobbers his opponent so quickly that he struts back into the dressing room barely spritzed with sweat. He reminds me of a cocky Salvador Dali who delivered the world's shortest speech. He stood up and said: *This speech will be so brief that I have already finished.*

Is Dino on a collision course with Tony?

Am I on a collision course with Dom?

8

COOL DOWN # 2

Boxing is like sin. It's too popular to be abolished.

—Dave Anderson

<u>Friday, March 12:</u>

The school bell rings. The White Plains High School hallway instantly swarms with adolescent traffic. Youthlet egos. Pubescent confusion. Mild madness. Throbbing hormones. Boners. I look at the pretty girls with budding breasts and wonder which ones have already experienced the big one.

Suddenly, someone taps my shoulder. Sing-Sing.

"We've got to talk." She escorts me into my classroom and shuts the door. "There's this girl, a sophomore…she's suicidal." Sing-Sing's beautiful face becomes etched in pain. "She's cutting herself. Knives, tin cans, anything sharp. She says it comforts her."

"So?"

"So…I don't know," she sighs. "I'm scared."

"Ask Todd Rapier. He has all the answers."

She's shaking her head. "No. We've implored her—we've practically tried to kiss her out of her darkness, but nothing's working. Every night she goes home and slices off pieces of her face."

"What?"

"With a razorblade. She slices off her pimples. Every morning she comes to school with fresh wounds."

"Speak with her parents, not me," I say.

"They're in denial." She touches my arm. "Todd and I are both hitting a wall. Please, you know how to talk to troubled kids. Speak with her."

"And say?"

In walks a girl. She's the isolat from the lunchroom. Her hair is still buzz cut on one side and pink on the other. Her sad 16-year-old face is pocked with oozing crusty red marks.

"Tina, meet Mr. Wood. He's a boxing coach."

"Hi." Her voice is barely audible, moth-like.

She's wearing army boots and ripped black fishnet stockings. Her bracelets and necklace are yellow police cordon tape that says CAUTION in black letters.

"How about if I drive you to Mr. Wood's boxing gym after school today?" smiles Sing-Sing.

Tina's brown eyes widen.

"Would you like that?" asks Sing-Sing.

"I dunno."

"C'mon, let's give it a try!" beams Sing-Sing.

Suddenly, Todd Rapier enters. He shoots Sing-Sing a meaningful glance. "I told you this wasn't a good idea." He looks at Tina and smiles. "Would you please excuse us, dear?"

Tina shuffles to the door.

"Tina," says Rapier, "forget whatever was said in here. I'll speak with your father tonight."

"My *father*? Who's he?" she murmurs.

"C'mon, Tina. You're all set for English Honors, remember?"

"Whatever," she says, disappearing out the door.

Rapier turns to Sing-Sing. "We went over this. Peter is excellent with low-level kids, but not Tina. She's brilliant."

"Brilliant and angry," says Sing-Sing.

"Sing-Sing, she was last year's eighth grade valedictorian…"

"A *sexually abused* eighth grade valedictorian."

"Exactly," says Rapier. "Now you want them to fist her *face*? She needs a shrink, not a punch in the nose."

"We're not helping her," says Sing-Sing.

"We *are* helping her," decrees Rapier.

"No, we're not," stamps Sing-Sing, "*We're* failing because *she's* failing. Look at her face!"

"She's in love with her depression," rationalizes Rapier. "Ultimately, she has the right to fail."

"Failure isn't an option," cries Sing-Sing.

"Yes it is," nods Rapier.

"It's true what everyone says about you," she nods. "You're callous."

"No. I'm realistic." Then Rapier turns to me. "People make choices. You're a coach. You see it all the time."

"Get out," I say. I hate how he's hiding his personal ambition behind a virtuous façade; I hate Sing-Sing falling for it; I hate the girl's sliced-up face.

Was Tina the same girl Scrawby wrote a love letter to last year? The girl who was fisted?

Saturday, March 13:

Dino orders a pair of black Ringside trunks. Great sign!…

Monday, March 15:

…but Dino didn't bother to come to the gym today.

Neither did Tina.

Stuttering Bobo is sitting nude on the locker room bench. He's back from a fight card in Atlantic City and he's rehashing his half hour of ecstasy with a Korean prostitute. "S-She brought me into this tiny room, laid me d-down on a rubbing-table, and give me a *dy-no-mite* blowjob. For an extra $10, she take off her bra so I could pinch her n-nipples."

"What color was her b-bra?" mimics Cockeye.

"B-Black. For an Asian, she had some real sweater m-meat, I ain't kiddin'!"

"What color was her panties?" asks Black Earl, scratching his jockstrap.

"Black. Them p-panties be so tiny, they like a piece o' lint!"

"How much she cost?" asks Tiger.

"H-Hundred fifty."

"Was she p-pretty?" mocks Cockeye.

Bobo thinks on that one. "Yeah, she was p-pretty…except for her face."

Tonight I get a letter in the mail. I don't know what to make of it.

Dear Coach Wood,

> *I wake up each morning extra extra early like*
> *each morning study for my GED. I'm gonna*
> *pass it. And I be working out real hard. Doing*
> *1,000 push ups each day.*

Sincerly,
Tyrone Crooks

P.S. I might be illigible for a early work-relese program.

P.S.S. I be looking u up.

Tuesday, March 16:

Dino walks in with his right arm in a sling.

"Oh, no," I moan.

"Door fell on my shoulder…Bad things always happen to me."

I take off his shirt, lay him down on the rubbing table, and I knead his muscular traps and deltoids for a good twenty minutes. It must've done the trick because he takes off his sling and works five good rounds on the floor.

After he showers, Dino points to a *Daily News* photo of a boxer with a lump of proud flesh below his left eye. "Kid's always talking trash. Says he'll meet me in the finals."

"Jihad Harris," I nod. (I scouted him; he's tough.) I hand him one of my last vials of Sing-Sing's ginseng. "Drink it. It cures shoulders."

At the end of the day, walking out the gym, Dino reminds me about his *three-day vacation to Pittsburgh for a ticket-agent seminar and he won't be back till Monday. Bye!*

Fine. Go, dickhead.

At 7:00, I get home and devour a whole box of Entenmann's Chocolate Cookies.

Monday, March 22:

"It was terrible," says Dino, returning from his Pittsburgh seminar. "Us back-room guys hate those ticket agents."

"Why?"

"They're phonies."

"You do road-work?" I ask. It's been six days.

Six days!

He shakes his head.

"Why not?"

He shrugs. *Asshole.*

We wait a half-hour for sparring. Suddenly, Stuttering Bobo pops in.

"Wanna spar?" I ask.

"S-Sure," he says, looking at his watch. "B-But not long. Got a d-date!"

Wearing street clothes, Bobo steps into the ring and boxes rings around Dino. Dino looks bored

"Great job, Bobo!" I say, handing him $20. "Have a good date."

I then walk up to Dino and run my finger under his armpit. I taste the salt. He's right—he's not running. "You're an atrocious piece of shit!"

His t-shirt, I notice, reads: DON'T WATCH HISTORY—MAKE IT! Dino, you're the fucking phony. You should've been sprinting in Pittsburgh until your legs puked.

Tuesday, March 23:

Dino is scheduled to box five two-minute rounds with Tiger, but after three, I yell, *"Get out!* I can't stomach watching you any more!"

I yank off his headgear and throw it to the floor. "You're moving like a zombie! Look, I'm backing off. What's inside your head? You probably think I'm pushing too hard, but I ain't pushing hard enough! You're *here* but you *ain't* here! Yesterday, you looked like shit and today you look worse! It hurts too much to see your talent go down the drain. Work six rounds on the bag and come back tomorrow, *if you want.*"

There's a wealth of poison inside Dino I'm not tapping into. So far, he only has three prevailing moods: sadness, commiseration and boredom.

Whether he fears success or fears failure, it doesn't matter. He's swallowing himself up. He might as well be shooting heroin. I'm sick and tired of psychoanalyzing him.

Tonight I'm phoning friends, and students, warning them not to come to Dino's next fight. I've finally lost confidence in him. I'll tell Malcolm: cancel all bets.

Thursday, March 25:

Fight night.
Tiger and I are in the gym waiting.
It's getting late…No call…No nothing.
Suddenly the door opens…

9

THE QUARTER FINALS

**The most beautiful fighting machine
I have ever seen.**

—Ernest Hemingway, on Joe Louis

"Sorry I'm late," says Dino, strolling in.

"Get in the damn car!" I yell.

Like last time, Dino seems relaxed. But is he? Is he secretly hoping his opponent gets hit by a bus on his way to the fight, or is he hoping *we'll* get hit?

Dino's bout is again in Brooklyn—the same parish.

Dino draws Jack McKnight, a tough New York City firefighter. McKnight, probably in his late 20's, has an ugly pockmarked face and red receding hair.

While I tape Dino's hands, I repeat our strategy: "Double-up your jab, find angles-speed beats him."

Dino nods. "Look at my hands," he chuckles, "they're shaking."
And they are. *A lot.*

"Jihad Harris was trash-talking on the draw line again," he says,
softly. "Kept chanting, 'From the slave ship to The Championship.'
McKnight told him to shut the fuck up."

As we climb the basement stairs, we are met by Dom Bufano and
Tony Malzone coming down. Dom's sweaty face looks cracked and
leathery, like a well-oiled catcher's mitt. Tony's swollen eye is beginning to shut. "We was robbed!" spits Dom.

Shit, there goes the last chapter of my book.

Artie Mendoza, the pasty Jew built like a #2-pencil, beat him.

"Sorry, Dom," I say.

"Politics," he fumes. "Watch the damn judges."

"Wait here," I tell Dino. I run upstairs to find the hare-lipped usher
from our last fight.

The *wizard-genius.*

"Do me a favor. When my boxer comes up, look into his eyes
and tell him he's gonna win." This is the quarterfinals, a place that
specializes in crushing a kid's dreams. Half of tonight's fighters will
lose. I don't want that happening to Dino.

I slip the *wizard-genius* $20.

The *wizard-genius* is waiting for us at the top of the stairs. He
peers into Dino's eyes, frowns, and walks away.

Dino doesn't have a long wait. Up in the ring a hairy Brooklyn beast
with thick bull neck knocks out his opponent with a tremendous wal-
lop in 40 seconds. The smack of the knockout punch hushes the
crowd, then they erupt in a load of ecstasy. Wish Dino hadn't seen,
or heard, it. The unconscious opponent oozes onto the canvas and
stays oozed. Crumpled in the corner, with his feet splayed beneath
his butt, he resembles an eviscerated chicken.

"The winner—Fatty Langford!"

I wonder what cup of mud Fatty crawled out of. He looks pre-lingual.

His wide nostrils, bulging buttocks and thick neck look prehistoric—it's like he was scraped off a cave wall. He has an ugly white dragon tattooed on his stomach and someone in the dressing room whispered that he's the great grandson of the immortal Boston Tar Baby—Sam Langford—a turn-of-the century black heavyweight who was denied the chance at the title because of his skin color. I believe it. Fatty looks like he's bred to fight—his knuckles practically drag on the floor.

Langford bounds up the aisle, spots Dino, and snarls. "I break you teeth!"

Dino's standing in the ring awaiting the bell. He's taking a deep pull of air through his nose and shaking out his arms. Composure at the right time seems to be one of Dino's special gifts. There's a stoic, Pre-Columbian dignity and strength in his almond eyes.

Clang!

McKnight advances. Dino side steps, feints and peppers McKnight with deft jabs. After a brief feeling-out period, Dino attacks and begins hitting him a ton. I get goosebumps. Ring savvy is an art form, a gift from God that flows from a fighter like melody flows from a musician. Ring savvy is a muse that runs through a fighter's body. It can't be taught. I could die of love watching him punch McKnight's face in. Dino is on fire. He has all the weapons—he's varied, secret and omniscient. If God was revealed to Dostoevski in seizures, why can't boxing serve as a portal to the beyond, or the unknown, to Dino?

Suddenly, Dino dips stepping in and lashes out with a nasty left hook that catches McKnight's jaw flush. McKnight drops. Sprawled onto the canvas in the ring lights, the fireman's red chest hair caught glows like monkey fur.

"ONE...TWO...THREE..."

I look across the ring at McKnight's trainer. I wonder how he feels knowing his red-haired boy will be knocked out in a few more seconds.

At eight, McKnight wobbles up, ten years older. Immediately he walks into a flourish of left hooks and a solid right-hand down the pipe. Down he goes.

"…SIX…SEVEN…EIGHT…"

He wobbles up. If there were a chicken-hawk flying in the room, it would've been circling McKnight's red hair. The ref stops it when McKnight stumbles and his arms get tangled in the ropes.

Dino runs to the corner and hugs me.

"I love you, man!" I blurt, stripping off his headgear. Again, I want the crowd to cherish this wonderful kid and heap their love and adulation upon him. I want them to recognize his brilliance and beauty. This blooming. And I want *him* to *feel* it, too.

Later, I overhear him tell reporters, "I wouldn't be here without my coach."

I needed that.

Dark wind whistles and squirms through the windows as Dino, Tiger and I drive back to White Plains after Dino's victory.

"That chunky monkey Langford *killed* his opponent!" gasps Tiger from the back.

There's a brief, uncomfortable hush.

Dino breaks the silence with a story:

"I met a murderer once…eight years ago…My girl and me were walking down Avenue A…

10

THE DINO DISCUSSION

I fought maybe 300, 400 fights, and every one was a pleasure.

—Sam Langford

…during my drug days. Hanging out the window, was this drug dealer. *Come on up*, he says. So we go up three flights …Dirty rat's nest…All of a sudden he starts yelling about his girl who won't sign his lease…We don't care, we just wanna cop…When my girl walks to the bathroom, the dude jumps up and says, *No it's too messy.* So he brings us to the roof… keeps yellin' about his girl. We finally copped and leave…

…Two months later, in the *Daily News,* I see his face on the front page…Killed his girlfriend. Chopped her up into cutlets. Fed her to the homeless."

"No wonder his bathroom was messy," says Tiger.

Dino nods his head. "Chopped her up in the bathtub."

Five minutes later, Tiger asks, "Did you say *human cutlets*?"

Dino nods.

Monday, March 29:

Human cutlets. Tonight, I find a brown unmarked package on my front porch. I rip it open. Inside are two VHS tapes. I pop one into my VCR. It's Fatty Langford knocking out an opponent. The second tape is Jihad Harris tko'ing a tough black kid.

Both Langford and Harris could easily carve Dino into a human cutlet.

Who gave me this? And why?

I rewind the tapes and view them again. And again. And again.

Langford has the appearance of a slow-thinking lip-mover, but has a certain low-level excellence. Is he really related to The Boston Tar Baby? His right hand could funeralize a horse.

Cocky Jihad Harris has more talent than Langford. He's slick and quick. He's more of a professional-amateur, or amateur-professional.

The other semifinalist is Artie Mendoza, the skinny Jew with the pimply nose. Him, I'm not concerned about. (Yet, he's beaten every *goy* and *svartza* put in front of him.)

Dino, there isn't much farther to go. Hold yourself together.

And study these tapes.

Who gave them to us?

Wednesday, March 31:

"Stomach hurts," complains Dino, walking into the gym.

Oh, no, here we go again.

But somehow, he manages to hold himself together. For his second consecutive day he boxes four rounds with Tiger and two with Stuttering Bobo. (I pay Tiger $25 for three rounds, but he insists on donating one.) In that last round, Dino's cheek cuts, but it's more of a broken blood vessel.

Dino smells victory.

He's starting to throw terrific double left hook-right uppercut combos, the type that knock out human teeth. Maybe germinating within his delicate brain tissue are spurts of confidence? Maybe he's beginning to believe he's worthy?

Thursday, April 1:

A third good day. Dino works six easy rounds and appears healthy.

"You're going to be fine," I reassure.

Most of the tough guys in this tournament have been eliminated by all the other tough guys. That's boxing—a sport that cannibalizes itself until only one guy is left standing.

Dino, don't self-destruct! The title is yours! *Ours.*

Tina, the girl with pink hair and blood-pocked face, comes in today. She's sitting alone in the corner watching Dino spar Stuttering Bobo. Her shoulders and head bob while she does her physics homework. She seems to be enjoying herself.

Friday, April 2:

At the beginning of my 4th period class, I have been holding a daily "Dino Discussion."

Today, our "Dino Discussion" veers off topic when Adam mentions that his father, a neurologist, works at Mt. Sinai Hospital. "Muhammad Ali came in years ago suffering from Parkinson's. My dad was one of the team doctors studying Ali's brain scan. He says the processing center of Ali's brain resembles a seven-year-old child's."

Zoe, my anti-boxing student, raises her hand. "Mr. Wood, why are you coaching such a dumb sport?"

The class awaits my answer.

"What do you get out of it?" she presses.

"Well, Zoe, I get to see a young man, like Dino, reach his goal."

"Here's what I think…I think you're getting an *old* man to reach *his* goal," she says. "I think you're doing this for *yourself.* I think you're re-living your Golden Gloves days through your fighter." It's a solid blow to my midsection.

"I've had the same thought, myself," echoes Diane. "Why else would you put up with Dino's lame excuses?"

I shake my head and wipe the pops of sweat from my forehead. "Every day I ask myself the same question," I admit. "In fact, yesterday, Dino got sick again."

The class moans.

"If you were in my shoes," I ask the class, "what would you tell Dino?"

"First, I'd ask him why's he always getting sick," says Heather, a thin girl sitting in the corner, who rarely speaks.

"Ask why he's such a quitter," volunteers Karen.

"Why is he copping out?" asks Stephen, a shy boy sitting in the back. "Doesn't he have faith in himself?"

"Perhaps not," I nod. "But he can find faith, can't he?"

Some students nod.

"Dino can pull this thing out. Can't he?"

"You mean *you* can pull it out," says Zoe. "No offense, Mr. Wood, but I still think this is all about *you*. I'm sure Dino's grateful, but you're projecting yourself onto him. That's what Ms. Tu says."

My eyes widen. "Oh?"

"She says you project yourself onto all your fighters."

"Let's open our books to page 86…"

Saturday, April 3:

Fight night.

Dino and I sit up front—Tiger and Black Earl sit in back. We're driving to the semi-finals in Queens at Lost Battalion Hall. The black squirming gusts of cold night air whistle from a small opening of Dino's window. It makes me queasy.

Black Earl mentions Langford's *fat comic-book ass*, then adds, "Did you know butt muscles are the strongest muscles in the human body?"

"Really?" says Tiger.

Earl nods. "John Wayne's autopsy showed he died with thirty pounds of shit in his intestines and a two-foot piece of solid oat bran was removed from his colon."

It's conversation.

We arrive early.

This time the dressing room is up one flight of rickety wooden stairs, which leads to a balcony overlooking the small ring. We sit in metal chairs, near the official's desk.

The number of fighters is thinning out. Even nationally-ranked Joey Hughes was tko'ed last night—on a cut. I look around at the fighters remaining. They're loosening up or drifting in and out of thin sleep. Or praying.

Waiting never gets easy. There's always a faint whiff of blood in the air: a competitive, primitive odor. I look around and realize that fighters are a tightly-knit community. I'm proud to be connected to them. We're the lucky ones—if we didn't have boxing, we'd be running down city streets hurling grenades into people's faces.

"MIDDLEWEIGHT DRAW!" bellows an official.

Dino walks into a small room with the three other semifinalists—cocky Jihad Harris, muscular Fatty Langford and scrawny Artie Mendoza...

...I'm hoping Mendoza...

...It's Fatty Langford. *Shit!*

We're the second fight.

Dino is stepping into his black boxing trunks. I'm taping him up; his hands are shaking.

I'm glancing over at Langford and notice his fat ass is still rooted to a wooden folding chair. He's still wearing a beige pantyhose do-rag on his nappy head and he has that flared-nostril look. He's obviously a toxic creature ruled by excessive testosterone. He looks scary, like he'd be more comfortable in the jungle wearing a penis-gourd. But he isn't getting dressed and I'm not sure why. He's just sitting there, inhaling and exhaling. The tropical Harlem wind from deep inside his massive chest is revving. He's either trying to psych Dino out by shooting him ghetto glares, or he's deciding the best way to break Dino's teeth.

Meanwhile, Jihad Harris is striding by us, holding a Bic razor. An official is ordering him to "Go shave off your damn goatee." (If he gets cut, stitching him up is easier.)

"Look at these idiots—they ain't ready to fight," I scoff.

Dino's somber face is quiet.

From the balcony we watch the first bout: Jihad Harris versus Artie Mendoza.

"My Lord!" cries Tiger. "Mendoza's awful!"

"Yeah, he's awful," I agree. "But he wins!"

As soon as I say it, Mendoza unloads a beautiful, well-timed right hand.

POW! Harris drops!

"The winner is…Artie Mendoza!"

I admit, the first time I had seen Mendoza pawing the heavybag at the initial weigh-in, he struck no fear in my heart, but now he's just made gefilte fish out of the cocky Jihad Harris and battered his way into the New York City Golden Gloves Finals!

It's Dino's big moment. He's bouncing up and down in his corner awaiting the bell. Thunder, lightning, snow, fire, his dead mother and father are churning through his head.

My heart is sweating.

The human-shaped object standing in the opposite corner, with the white dragon tattoo on his belly, is frothing at the mouth.

Clang!

11

THE SEMI FINALS

He hit me on the top of my head and I thought the roof had caved in.

—Gunboat Jones, on the punching power of Sam Langford

Langford sprints across the ring. He's frantic. He's muscular. He's wild.

Dino sidesteps.

Langford's brains are, primarily, in his right hand. You can tell he has a God-given killer instinct, but Dino's too fast and nimble. Dino is a combination of Middleweight Champ Roy Jones and a machine gun. Jabs jump into Langford's fat lips—he eats each punch.

Langford's thick arms swish and swoosh air. Dino throws two solid right hands over the top and connects with both. *Smack. SMACK!*

Dino takes the first round handily.

"How you feel?" I ask, swabbing him down.

"Good!"

"Jab, jab, jab and throw the left-hook," I instruct. "But watch his right!"

Clang!

Langford leaps forward. His squat musculature is sparked with adrenaline and animal revenge. Unlike the other fighters, he's not intimidated by Dino's cut physique. Suddenly, he explodes a beautiful right hand onto Dino's jaw. Dino sags. Langford is instantly in a frenzy pounding four more crushing rights onto Dino's head. With each clout, Langford grows crazier. Punching, he's ventilating his entire being, down to his bowels. He is an insane paroxysm of violence. Dino holds tight. The only thing that scares a guy like Langford is to punch his ugly face for two minutes, and Dino isn't doing it. Dino's slick movement, jabs, and quickness are gone.

Clang!

Dino lost that round *big.*

Dino slumps down, puffing.

"C'mon! Suck it up!" I implore. "You need this round, Dino!"

Dino's mouth is gulping the smoky air. His chest is heaving.

Clang!

Langford storms from his corner stripped of frills. He's 165 pounds of human momentum. He's full of rage and hope. An obvious psychopath, Langford's determined to detonate the mother of all bombs on Dino's pretty face. Half-man and half-ape, he whizzes punches from all directions. These missiles, curving through the smoky air, leave stretch marks. Langford is thriving on his own hostility, but Dino is somehow able to lean back and make most of Fatty's punches miss his jaw by inches.

The Chunky Monkey plods forward. Suddenly, he knocks Dino into a neutral corner with a looping right to the mouth. He now has Dino where he wants—pinned to the ropes. Dino's tired. He can't hide. It's toe-to-toe. A slugfest.

Bad idea. This brawling trench warfare is exactly Fatty's fight. Punch after punch sinks into Dino's face. But, suddenly, how do you describe it, the change that comes over Dino? Out of the mysterious resource of his will, comes vitality. Suddenly, somehow, Dino does the impossible…he grabs Fatty's elbow, spins him, and sidesteps to the right. Now Langford's on the ropes! Something buried deep surges up within Dino. He measures Fatty and starts plowing lefts and rights into his face. Fatty's eating every punch! Langford doesn't have the ring savvy, or energy, to turn it around. With Dino's sudden resurgence, Fatty seems to wilt. He crouches and holds as Dino uppercuts and hooks. At the bell, Dino lands a solid left hook to Langford's jaw. *Crack!* It sounds so beautiful!

As the ref collects the judges' scorecards, I towel off Dino's red sweaty face. His ribs are still heaving with exhaustion.

Langford, mouth hung open and panting, shuffles over and embraces Dino. "Goo figh."

"Goo figh," mutters Dino.

Both boys just stand there, arms limp, exhausted. I douse them both with water from my bottle. I bet, together, they've lost five pounds of water weight. And 100 pounds of anger.

The announcer grabs the mic…

…"THE WINNER IN THE BLUE CORNER…DINO LAZARO!"

Dino reaches towards the sky with both hands.

Langford shuffles back to his corner.

Back in the dressing room, Dino slumps into a chair, buries his face in his taped hands, and sobs.

"Let it go," I whisper, kneading the back of his neck. It's a good, healthy sob. His body is shaking. I'm kneeling before him and begin crying myself. I guess this is what's called a bittersweet moment—he reaches the finals, the proudest moment in his life, and the people he loves the most are dead. I brush a tear from my eye. "Hey, the size of the tear is the size of the love."

Suddenly, I'm feeling nervous. I'm uncomfortable with intimacy—especially with someone who reminds me so much of myself. "Be right back. I'm phoning in your win to the paper. You be okay?"

He nods, wiping his eyes.

I start walking away but, suddenly—*Wham!*—something invisible, and potent, stops me: it's the thought of Dino being alone at this poignant, precious moment. It kills me, absolutely kills me. I go back and ruffle his hair. Plus I hug him about four hundred times.

I'm looking for a payphone, outside. Beneath the elevated train, standing alone in the dark is Jihad Harris. The whites of his eyes are flecked with serious blood clottage and his facial injuries look automobile-related. I try to cheer him, but a crushed dream is a crushed dream and like I said, the semifinals is an emotional blood-bath—a place that specializes in crushed dreams.

All these fighters believe that if only they can reach the finals, their miserable lives will instantly change for the better. All it takes is a little roadwork and a lucky right hand and their self-worth will dramatically flourish and all self-doubt will be wiped out forever. All they need to do is reach the finals in Madison Square Garden. Therein lies perfect happiness.

I can't sleep. Tossing and turning, just lying there in the dark tracing with my eyes, over and over again, where the wall meets the ceiling

Finally I pick up the phone and dial…

Why am I doing this?…

…My stomach tightens…

…A trickle of sweat runs through my hair…

…"Hello, Sing-Sing?"…

12

THE FINALS

I don't care what religion he is. If he doesn't get moving, he's gonna lose the fight.

—Gil Clancy, after being told Howard Davis was a vegetarian

"Hi!...Peter?" There seems to be a smile in her voice, even though it's 1:00 am.

I tell her how Tina's been visiting the gym, how she sits there doing her homework, how she seems happy. I tell her about Dino reaching the finals.

"Very impressive." Yes, that's *definitely* a drowsy little smile in her voice.

"Yeah, well, I never see you in school anymore."

"I've been busy, she says softly. Lesson plans. The after-school program,"

I so much want to reach out and share this moment with her. I don't want to be alone.

"Well, best of luck with Dino," she says, "go to sleep"

Monday, April 5:
    Dino's fight is in eleven days. Why isn't he here?
    I call. No answer.
    I drive to his house.
    I knock.
    Silence.
    I tuck this fight plan into the mailbox:

The Artie Mendoza Fight Plan

1) Mendoza always finishes strong.
***Dino->** Break his spirit—win the first round.*
2) Mendoza punches for three rounds—has excellent stamina.
***Dino->** Punch faster and stronger. Be in Aaron-Pryor-shape! (He will be!)*
3) Mendoza needs range to punch.
***Dino->** Go inside his range and throw three-punch combos.*
4) Mendoza will stalk you.
***Dino->** Meet him with an overhand-right. He'll walk into it—then quickly follow-up with fast combos inside.*
5) Mendoza is a smart fighter.
***Dino->** You are smarter and more experienced. Don't lose focus.*
6) Mendoza is deceptively good—he wins. (He beat Joe Shaw, Tony Malzone and Jihad Harris!)
***Dino->** You are the best fighter. Prove it!*
7) Mendoza rises to the occasion.
***Dino->** You'll rise to the occasion. Remember: your goal is not to reach the finals. It is to **WIN** the finals.*
8) Mendoza throws a wide left hook off the jab; he'll also throw the left upper-cut.
He throws a straight right.
He throws a one-two.

He throws the one-two-three.
He headhunts…
Dino-> *You're a much* better boxer.
You punch harder and faster.
You are more experienced.
You are physically stronger.
You deserve to win!

9) Mendoza, the nice, sweet seventeen-year-old kid who politely shook your hand is **politically linked**. If he can't beat you physically or mentally, he'll beat you **politically**.

Dino-> *Don't allow the fight to go the distance!*

10) Mendoza gets more confident as the fight progresses.

Dino-> *Be aggressive and set the pace.*

11) Mendoza will try to back you up throwing feather. If he does, he wins.

Dino-> *You must meet him coming in with your overhand-right; throw combos which will* **break his spirit or knock him out.**

Tuesday, April 6:

Where's Dino?

I phone his home. On the fifth try, someone answers.

"Ain't feelin' good," rasps a voice.

"Dino? Is that you?"

"Uh-huh…"

"What's wrong?"

"Throat…wrist."

"Well, you got to pull it together," I say, softly. "Your fight's in ten days."

"Miss my parents…," he says, softly.

"They're here," I say. "They're with you now."

"Coach…I kneel by my bed each night and pray…*Mother, you're my left and Father, you're my right.*"

"They've been with you all along. I feel your father's presence."

"Daddy was tough…Mom was quiet…She guides me from above…Dad pushes from behind…Coach?"

"Yeah?"

"My mom committed suicide…" *Click.*

Wonderful…I envision Dino lying between two white sheets slitting his wrists with a razor blade.

I recently read about an Indian doctor who works with autistic children, kids so profoundly frail and withdrawn that when they stand up, they fall—just plop over, without shielding their faces. This doctor discovered that if he stretches a rope from one side of the room to the other and puts the rope in the kids' hands, they'll walk across the room without falling. Over the months he stretches thinner and thinner rope, until he's using something nearly invisible, like fishing line, and these fragile kids can still walk across the room without falling. Later, the doctor cut the fishing line into little pieces, and as long as the kids held on to their line, they can walk without falling.

That's what Dino needs—emotional fishing line.

Wednesday, April 7:

Dino comes in sucking a red throat lozenge. He trains lightly; his sweat drops are now dime-sized. I'm not so sure anymore if that's good or bad. He gets absolute obedience from the peanut bag as local press and photographers snap pictures.

But I'm extremely wary. I hug him. "Sorry about your mom," I whisper.

He nods.

Tina is sitting in a chair in her favorite corner. She's comfortably curled up in a chair, sitting on her graffitied sneakers. Every day she quietly does her homework. Today it's math. Every so often, she looks up at my fighters. Especially Dino. If it weren't for her chopped off zits, half-shaved head, and pink hair, she'd be quite pretty.

Thursday, April 8:

Eight days left.

There's no one for Dino to spar today, so I move with him three easy rounds; then he hits the heavybag for three.

Suddenly his face twists in pain. "AARRGH! My thumb!"

By now, I expect this nonsense. "Run tonight," I say, gently. "Blood will circulate through your thumb and heal it like new. *You're gonna be fine, Dino.*"

At the end of his workout, Dino fishes into his dufflebag and hands me his four complimentary fight tickets. "Here."

"How about your friends?"

He shakes his head.

"How about a girl?"

He frowns, coughing.

This kid's so alone. So fragile.

"I'll take one," says a thin voice. It's Tina, hopping out of her chair and standing beside us. "I'd love to go," she says.

Dino hands her two tickets.

"But if you don't want to give them to me," she says, "I'll understand."

He presses them into her palm.

Tina smiles big. "Thanks!"

Dino stares at her red-blotched face.

"My face, right?" Tina shrugs. "I was stupid once."

"Yeah," he nods. "me, too."

Tina points with her chin to the ring. "You're awesome."

He smiles big.

"I want to learn," she says, "but my father won't let me."

At the end of dinner at Red Lobster, Dom Bufano hands me a brown paper bag. "Another gift," he says. Inside is videotape of Tony Malzone's loss to Artie Mendoza.

"So, it was *you!*"

"Don't say I never gave you nothin', honky."

"Why you always call me *honky*?"

"'Cause that's what you is, honky!" He laughs.

Paying the check, I say, "Your boy Malzone lost, but you performed a miracle with him."

"Yeah, he can be proud of hisself."

"He came a long way from eating outta garbage cans."

Dom's eyes twinkle. "Didn't believe that, did ya? He never ate outta no garbage can."

"What?"

He grins.

"It wasn't true?"

"Nah! Tony be a preppy from Westchester! He's high class!"

"You lying sonofabitch. Why'd you lie?"

"To scare your boy, " he beams.

I look at his old grinning face.

"Best liar wins. Remember? Probably couldn't find that in your college books."

Friday, April 9:

"Total bull!" shouts Todd Rapier, striding into the teacher's room. He slams his briefcase on the table.

"Todd," says Sing-Sing, following him, "it might be a very good idea."

"Nonsense! If I want her educa-babble, I'll ask for it."

"What's wrong?" asks Mike Donahue, an English teacher, looking up from *Hamlet*.

"Nothing's wrong!" jabs Rapier.

"Tell him, Todd," says Sing-Sing.

"*You* tell him, Miss *Genius*," he snaps, slamming down his *The New York Times*.

"Todd's upset." explains Sing-Sing. "The principal just ordered us new workbooks for our after-school program. I think they're fine, but Todd…"

"Disagrees!" Rapier blurts. "She's shoving crap down my throat."

"What's the book?" asks Mike.

"Anger Management," says Sing-Sing.

"What's wrong with anger management?" asks Mike.

"That's just great, Mike!" he shouts. "Remember *The Three Rs?*— *Reading, Writing, and Arithmetic*? Well, the new *Three Rs* are—*Reproduction, Racism, Recycling*. And now we have a fourth—*Rage!*" He kicks the table.

"Who's teaching this anger management course?" asks Mike.

I swivel my neck and aim my face at Rapier. "*You?*"

The room explodes with laughter. Convulsive belly laughter. Hilarity. Guffawing. Teachers, one by one, point their fingers at Rapier and chant, "*You?*"

"*You?*"

"*You?*"

His arrogant face is flushed with embarrassment. I now realize who he really is: my supercilious stepfather. It feels so good to see them both stride out the door. But the best thing is Sing-Sing—she's laughing too, so hard, she's wiping back tears.

It's beautiful what one punch can achieve.

Monday, April 12:

Dino's in high spirits, hitting the pads hard. Despite his "sprained thumb" he's really plugging.

"Throw the right to the belly *hard*," I bark. "Harder! Harder!"

He winces in pain. "My thumb!"

I hand him two aspirins and tell him to shadow box. Tomorrow he spars—sprain or no sprain. Whether you're a brain surgeon, pianist, or boxer, you've got to practice.

On my way home, I drive past the Westchester County jail and envision Tyrone Crooks lying on his cot inside his jail cell; his brain is rotting in his skull. Jail's his choice. Life must have been too painful for him. But alone, inside a jail cell, he can invent his reality. And he can blame everyone else for his problems.

Tuesday, April 13:
Three days left.

Thumb is fine. Dino boxes four three-minute rounds with Tiger and for the first time in a long time, he digs deep and shows me roughness. He's beginning to see the light at the end of the tunnel. He says he studies the Mendoza tape every night.

"Good, but don't make him into some monster. *You're* the monster." I flip him a vial of Sing-Sing's ginseng. "Drink it. It'll heal your thumb."

Wednesday, April 14:
I pick up Tiger at the Mobil station on the hutch. I pat his back. "We're in the finals because of *you.*"

"No, Coach. You're in the finals because of The Lord," he corrects.

"Maybe. But The Lord isn't Dino's sparring partner."

An hour later Tiger and Dino are moving around in the ring, cautiously. In the first round, Dino winces. "OW!"

I tie his gloves tighter.

He continues to spar four great rounds and looks even better than yesterday. His movement is sharp and crisp and he actually nails Tiger with a right haymaker.

"What'll work on Mendoza?" I ask.

"Anything I do," he smiles.

At the end of the day, in the locker room, I find another wet girl lying on top of a green locker. She's a beautiful redhead squatting over a man. She's peeing on his bald head.

When Tiger steps out of the shower, I hold it up for him to see. "Recognize her?"

He laughs.

"She yours?"

He towels off, laughing.

"Well, whose is she?" I ask.

"Well, ain't sure, but I got an idea. I once saw Bobo stuffin' a picture down his trunks."

"Bobo?"

"Stuffs 'em into his jock before he works out. He likes a girl's face down there."

"Weird."

"That's why they be wet."

We both laugh.

Suddenly, I fish into my back pocket and hand Tiger an envelope.

He drapes his wet towel around his neck. "What's this?"

"Open it at home."

Sparring payment: $500.

Thursday, April 15:

Dino walks into the gym office asking for adhesive tape for his hands.

"Sit down," I say, looking up from *Ring* magazine.

He slumps to the floor.

"Why do you always sit on the floor?" I ask.

He shrugs.

I slide down, next to him, shoulder to shoulder. "Why not use a chair?"

He looks puzzled.

"You're still 11 years old, aren't you?" I say, softly. "You're still back there with your mom and dad."

He looks at me weird.

"Dino…why are you here?" I ask.

"The Gloves," he says.

"To *win* The Gloves!" I correct. "But, *why* do you want to win The Gloves?"

"Why?"

Silence.

"I'll tell you why. You entered this tournament because of him."

He looks confused.

"Sure, you're doing this for you, but you're also doing this for *him*." I hand him a roll of adhesive tape. "Since you were 78 pounds, your dad taught you stance, jab and right hand. It was his gift of love. Now, you're the beautiful fighter he always wanted. Tomorrow night, a packed crowd of 6,000 people will admire your artistry. Your father did something very special—he planted the seeds of beauty within you. Honor that."

He's looking into his lap, twisting the adhesive tape around his forefinger.

"Dino, what motivates you?"

He shrugs.

"Anger? Pain? Hate? Shit's squirming inside you, but there's something else…"

"What?"

I shove him playfully. "C'mon, guess."

He shakes his head.

"You have no idea?"

"No."

"Love. It's the strongest motivation you got. You love your mom and you love your dad and, because you love them, you're going to kick Mendoza's butt! You're in that ring, first and foremost, because of love."

Is this sinking in?

"Dino, tomorrow night, you're going to flower…like a tulip!"

Before they leave the gym, I hand Stuttering Bobo, Black Earl and Cockeye sealed envelopes: $200 each.

I step into the Cage office to speak with Malcolm. "Tomorrow night you'll get your Golden Gloves Champ."

"You sound confident," he says, looking up from his computer.

"I am," I nod. "Place your bets."

He laughs. "Me? Bet? Never!" He wheels away from his computer. "I have something for you." He holds up a piece of paper. "Been working on this for months. Just came through. It's a college scholarship. For Dino. Ten thousand dollars."

"Ten thousand dollars?"

"Win or lose," he smiles.

"Why?" I ask.

"Why?" he repeats, squinting. "Because White Plains helps kids. That's why." He shakes his head. "But I still hate boxing."

13

MADISON SQUARE GARDEN

The boxing public generally are a blood-thirsty lot. They like to see a good hard fight, and if there's plenty of gore and snot flying around they love it.

—Henry Cooper, British Heavyweight Champ

Friday, April 16:

Fight night.

We're driving down the West Side Highway and the cold dark Hudson River, on our right, is slowly rolling south. Cold wind is whooshing and wheezing outside and thin anorexic raindrops are chaffing the car windows. It's quiet inside the car, except for Dino's rumbling stomach.

New York City begins where green trees end.

At 79th Street, I point to a crow that seems to be retching on the side of the highway.

I point. "Bird's puking."

"Nah,…choking," mutters Dino.

Oh, no. Winning this bout will be the hardest thing Dino will ever do and he better be thinking straight.

"You cut your fingernails last night?" I ask. It's less weight on his hands.

He nods.

"And toenails?"

He nods.

A bug splats on the windshield. I point and grin. "Mendoza!"

He smiles back. I *think* it's a smile.

It's a quiet drive. The tempo of our hearts are beating together. He doesn't want to talk. I play upbeat music—*Jockjams.*

We swing down into the mouth of the Madison Square Garden parking lot on 32nd Street. The attendant hands me a stub.

"See this kid?" I point. "He's the next Golden Gloves middleweight champion!"

"Oh, really?" But the man doesn't seem impressed. Instead, he points to the front of my front headlight. "Blown out."

I don't want to prolong Dino's pre-fight stress by hanging around Madison Square Garden, so I've arranged an early weigh-in. A few boxers are already there, a Spanish flyweight and a drowsy-looking black heavyweight with a deep vertical facial scar from forehead to chin. Then we take a taxi to my friend's midtown apartment to rest.

My friend, Max, is a Vietnam War hero suffering from post-combat syndrome. Max: he's a great guy but, unfortunately, he's mental. He's on permanent disability and will do crazy things when stressed, like pick fights with cab drivers, or provoke arguments with waiters and cashiers. He's 55 but still shaves his head like an 18-year-old Marine grunt in boot camp.

We meet Max in his lobby and the three of us walk up First Avenue to a steak joint for lunch. The weather's *drismal.* On the way, Max motions to Dino, "So this is the head-banger, huh?"

"Sshh!" I don't think Dino heard.

"He seems like the quiet type," says Max.

I nod.

Max smiles. "That's cool. Serenity's the vessel in which violence should be stored."

At the restaurant, Dino hardly touches his pre-fight meal: salad, sliced beef, potatoes, and peas. Water. No butter.

"Waitress," I say, "here's the next New York Golden Gloves middleweight champion."

She smiles and winks. Dino's handsome face remains deadpan.

We walk leisurely back to Max's apartment, ride up the elevator, and enter his one-bedroom apartment.

"Dino, lie down and relax," suggests Max, pointing to a soft, gray mattress lying in the middle of the hardwood floor. "Try her out. She's Margaret, my masseuse."

Dino lies down.

"Take off your shoes; close your eyes," insists Max. He then plays one of his soothing, therapeutic tapes—a waterfall. "All you need now is to dull your mind into a quiet desert and call it *peace*," he whispers. "You want *in*tense without being tense."

I love Max, but the poor man is mildly deranged. He kicks off his shoes and strips off his shirt, revealing a half-finished tattoo—a large black battleship sailing on his chest. He sits back on his soft couch, closes his eyes and espouses his new life philosophy. "After Vietnam, I've been on a spiritual path. I love everyone. I try to see the good in every person and I try to be caring and understanding and give the benefit of doubt to every one I meet, especially to those people I like. And the people I don't like, they can go suck my cock."

POP! A light bulb in the lamp beside Dino blows.

"Damn it!" shouts Max, stamping his bare feet to the floor. "Nothing goes right! First, it's my ex-wife, then my meds, now this! Aw, screw it!"

"Nah," says Dino, propping himself on his elbows, "it's me...third bulb I popped this week."

Suddenly, I remember my blown headlight—on Dino's side. Is this psychic energy? A poltergeist? Bad karma? A coincidence?

There are no accidents.

Max hails a cab for Madison Square Garden. "Hey, cabby!" he shouts. "See this kid? He's the next Golden Gloves middleweight champion! He's a real head-banger!"

I cringe. Dino's face remains blank.

We climb into the cab and head for The Garden. I wonder if Dino is looking for *signs.* Fighters are highly superstitious. Nino Valdez, a heavyweight contender in the '60s, had a strange ritual before his fights. Before driving to the arena, he'd make his trainer stop at a nearby river so he could throw all of his training equipment into the water. Jose Torres, a light heavyweight champion, was spooked by seeing a white towel draped on a ring rope the day of a fight.

We're walking through the bowels of the legendary Madison Square Garden with our dufflebags. It's a labyrinth of narrow, white, concrete corridors. Bright fluorescent lighting. Gray concrete floor. We're the first ones in the "Blue" dressing room—a concrete cubicle with a tiny shower and bathroom with shiny chrome fixtures.

Now, the stress of waiting.

I'm flipping through tonight's fight program, looking at all of the tough mug shots of the finalists. There's Dino—big brown eyes, straight black hair, high cheekbones and blank stare.

No, these young men are not herky-jerky street urchins, personality disorders or twisted outcasts—they're winners. They've done it; they've reached the finals. Sure, there are sad stories: Sandy Saddler, the great featherweight champion of the '40s and '50s, standing on a street corner signing his autograph—a straight line. Or Aaron Pryor, shadowboxing for nickels. Or heroic Joe Louis standing on a chair in a hotel bedroom smearing mayonnaise on the cracked ceiling trying to seal out poisonous gas from the killers above.

Artie Mendoza is the lone white face. He looks weaselish—a bit like Herbie Pish. Suddenly, my eyes bulge! Under his photo, I read: *Kid Gloves Champion; Currently the Junior Regional Champion.* No wonder he kept winning—he's a ringer!

Damn! I have to re-learn what Dom Bufano already taught me: never judge a guy by appearance.

At 7:00, an unexpected character from Dino's past sticks his head into the dressing room. It's Petey—Dino's former trainer from twelve years ago! Petey's a short, edgy man of about 35. Dino smiles and seems happy to see him, so I let him stay. It passes time; we're the 17th fight.

"I been following you in the *Daily News*," says Petey. "Here, I brought *unos fotos.* Here's you at eight years old. And here's your old fight card. You be 4'9."

I look at Dino's photo card. It's a young, scared face. (And, sure enough, he didn't have 100 fights—he had six.)

"Remember that time me, you, and *su padre* drive all the way to Ohio State Fair to fight?" says Petey.

Dino smiles wistfully.

"I lost track of you after, you know, your parents…"

Dino nods.

"*Su madre*…she love you *mucho*…"

During a lull in their conversation, I bring Dino into the corridor, where we can be alone one last time. "You came to me with a *dream*—to win The Gloves. Nothing's as real as this dream. The world changes, people die, but your dream won't die. Dreams stick with you—they link you with the guy you were yesterday and the guy you'll be tomorrow. Your dream links you to your mom and dad. Understand?"

He nods.

"Follow that dream. That's success. Now kick Mendoza's bony ass."

But my job's not done…There's still one piece of unfinished business that needs to be completed…

Dino and Mendoza sit ringside…we fight next. I'm sitting between them to absorb the tension.

It's a packed house—6,000 screaming boxing fans. This is the center of the universe. It's electricity, cigarette smoke, hooting and shouting—the rarified air of Madison Square Garden.

Heights scare me.

Dino should murder Mendoza. This bout should to be a *performance* not a *contest*—a mismatch on the scale of *ANT* versus *HEEL*.

But Mendoza, I suspect, is deranged. He could also be a functional schizophrenic for all we know. But he's sane enough to be a regional New York champ. He's walking into the ring a champ—a huge psychological edge.

I notice Vic Zimet, his trainer, smearing Vaseline all over Mendoza's face.

"Hey, Vic, that ain't allowed," I say.

"Mind your own fucking business," he blurts.

"It's against the rules!"

"Worry about your own fuckin' fighter," he says, slopping it on thick.

Dino and I are escorted to ringside.

"Good luck!" says a high-pitched voice. It's Mike Tyson. He pats Dino's robe. Donald Trump, the pretty woman beside him, Lennox Lewis, and Norman Mailer are staring at us. Mailer points.

Dino is oblivious. He simply walks up the steps into the flood lights.

The ref walks over to check us out.

"Check Mendoza's face," I point. "It's loaded with Vaseline. Make him take it off."

The ref glares. "I'll be the ref. Besides, your fighter's got some on, too."

"That's baby oil."

He points at my nose. "Keep it up, I'll disqualify you."

"You kiddin' me? Look at Mendoza's damn face! It's coated!"

"Dat's strike two…"

Fuck off! Dom's right—they're protecting the white boy—*politics.*
I turn to Dino and look into his red-rimmed eyes. "You ready?"

"Coach…" he says, softly. He puts his gloved hands on my shoulders. "Remind me why I'm here."

Whoa! Kid's sinking! Should I say he's fighting for *himself,* or for his *parents?*

"SECONDS OUT!"

Parents or himself?…"Do it for *yourself.* Break Mendoza's fucking teeth!"

Sweat is streaming down his cheeks, chest and arms.

"SECONDS OUT!"

"Feint and throw your right!" I whisper. I peer into his glassy eyes. His *eyeballs* are sweating. No…I look closer. He's crying. My crazy, sonofabitch middleweight is *crying!*

Clang!

14

THE FIGHT

"We?
Me!"

—Peter Wood, a poem inspired by Muhammad Ali

Mendoza stalks forward. He's not so much technique as attitude—less skill than will -- exactly what will beat Dino. Dino's side-stepping and dancing, flicking little nimble jabs. Each punch slides off Mendoza's face. They're like harmless moths brushing Mendoza's Vaselined cheeks. Halfway through the round, Dino's mouth is hanging open, it appears he might pass out from exhaustion. But he keeps moth-pecking Mendoza's with little pussy jabs. Suddenly Mendoza feints and careens a hard left-right onto Dino's head. Dino sags and clinches. At the bell, Dino stumbles back to the stool.

He sits dog-tired, panting. I sponge his face. He has that wired, eye-popping look.

"Lost that round," I say, kneeling before him. "Can't trust these judges. Gotta take next round."

His mouth is gulping air.

Clang!

Mendoza *miketysons* forward. Dino gets a second wind and begins popping him sharply, smartly. Mendoza's Vaseline face starts to resemble a child's well-spanked bottom. Dino's on his toes, dancing. He's peppering Mendoza's red, pimpled nose at will. Sparring Tiger has paid off. Mendoza's not slick like Tiger, or rough like Joey Hughes, but he keeps coming. Like a shark. Like a champ. Dino's jab-jab-jabbing and skip-skip-skipping around the ring. But everything he throws is sliding off Mendoza's slippery face.

Suddenly, Mendoza clobbers Dino's jaw flush. Dino's legs turn rubber. The crowd erupts.

Clang!

"You okay?"

Then it happens. Dino starts gasping wildly for air as if at high altitude. He has that exhausted look he gets before quitting. "Headgear's slippin' into my eyes! I can't…," he gasps.

"SHUT UP!" The liquid on my eyeballs burns. I see he's begging for defeat, it would be such a great relief when it finally arrived.

"I can't…"

I haul off and slap his face hard, just like his father. "LISTEN, DAMN YOU! One more round! Take him out! You're not a quitter!" Dino's more frightened than hurt or tired—he's suffering from imagination, not reality.

"I can't!" he gasps.

I slap him again, hard.

I hate heights.

Clang!

I lift him up by the elastic waist of his trunks and push him out. "Do it for *him*!" I yell.

Mendoza begins pounding Dino's face. Mendoza has stopped trying to figure out the complex butterfly dancing before him. Now he just chases and punches. That's how you win a fight, you punch.

Mendoza is drowning in adrenaline, swinging his arms wildly like an insane mental patient. And he's landing everything he throws. The ref looks like he's about to stop it. Dino, bleeding from his nose, looks down at me. I wave him on. The crowd, stamping, senses knockout.

So does Mendoza. He dogs forward with his left held low, exposing his jaw. Dino sees it and stops dancing—this is his chance. He plants his feet and throws a thunderous right at Mendoza's face. But it's a trap. Mendoza shifts his head six inches and Dino's right sails by Mendoza's ear. Mendoza counters with his own right. *Whap!*

Dino lands flat on his back.

"ONE... TWO... THREE... "

He rises to a knee and shakes his head.

"FOUR... FIVE... SIX... "

Dino's eyes aren't at home. He shakes away the cobwebs and gazes into the crowd. People are screaming with delight. A be-whiskered man, frantic in the aisle, shrill and manic, bellows, "GET UP! GET UP!"

Dino blinks...

"SEVEN... EIGHT... NINE... "

...he stands.

The ref peers into Dino's wide eyes and waves the fighters together.

Mendoza smells victory and attacks. But something in Dino clicks. He digs down, and digging down in boxing is the way to rise up.

He catches Mendoza coming in with an arcing right hand—the same punch that so impressed Dom in the gym. Mendoza's legs wobble. Dino bores in. A fierce double left-hook makes Mendoza's liver quiver. But Mendoza stays upright. Dino's beginning to surge, rocking in a big way. Punch after punch, he rolfs Mendoza's face. He's slamming him with wicked barrages as gobs of Vaseline fly off Mendoza's red face. Dino is boxing his life. His whole shattered life is finally spewing out through his fists—his dead parents, his drugged background, his criminal past, his bleak future. He's punching as he has never punched before, or will ever have to again. It's a thick, unconscious, primitive blood-daze.

Mendoza's nose is gushing blood.

Dino's beautiful, articulate punches are smashing into Mendoza's face. Mendoza's nose, jaw and cheeks are splattered with blood. But Mendoza is tough—he keeps coming, throwing bombs. Dino is getting nailed hard. Both kids are now in a moonlit area beyond scared. It's hard to tell their slamming punches in the ring from the pounding heartbeats in my chest. But what the fuck…their close-quarters slugfest is brutal, if not pretty. Blood is flying. It's two vicious mammals maiming each other, and the hollering crowd is loving it.

At the ten-second buzzer, I hold my breath. Various disaster scenarios flash through my mind—Dino getting caught with a desperate last punch or Dino losing on a foul. Suddenly, Dino pushes Mendoza off with his left shoulder and throws a vicious right uppercut. Dino's power surges from the ball of his right foot, to his hip, to his shoulder, to his fist, to Mendoza's jaw.

THUD!

It's like hitting a guy with the meat of a baseball bat. Mendoza's Vaselined headgear slips off and his sweaty head slams the ring post.

Clang! Clang! Clang!

Dino is gasping for air. I'm unbuckling his headgear. I think he won.

"You lost," quips the referee gliding past us, collecting the judges' cards.

In disbelief, we stare at his sweaty back as he glides away. Six steps later, he turns, and winks.

"You got it! You got it!" I beam.

The announcer grabs the mike dangling from a long black cord descended from the ceiling. Clears his throat…

"…*And the winner is…in the blue corner…Dino Lazaro!*"

I run into the ring and did what I had planned to do from the very first day I had met him—I lift him high in the air. "Raise your arms!" I yell. I can feel happiness and liberation pulsing from his chest, his lungs, his soul.

All your suffering has paid off, Dino.

The referee then approaches Dino and whispers, "Son, see me after the show."

Back in the dressing room, Petey somehow gets his grubby claws on Dino's beautiful diamond-studded Golden Gloves necklace and is attempting to fit it around Dino's neck.

"NO!" I bark. "*I* put them on, not you." I grab the gloves and marvel at the gleaming, glistening diamond winking between two golden gloves. Even though they'll never go around my neck, I momentarily feel 18-years-old again—only surer of myself. And smarter.

I encircle my arms around Dino's neck and clasp it on.

"Hey, honky! You lucked out!" grins Dom Bufano, punching my arm. "You couldn't a never done it without me."

"You're right," I say, hugging him.

"Maybe in twenty years you'll be smart enough to really coach." Then he shakes Dino's hand. "Fine work, son. You're one hell-of-a fighter, despite that honky." Then Dom calls me over. "Look, Pete, if ya wanna coach full-time, I got an opening. I'll take ya back. Love to have ya."

I smile but shake my head no. Somehow, Dom's offer reminds me of a straightjacket.

Our referee slithers into our dressing room. "Lazaro? I'm puttin' you on my next show…"

"Excuse me," I interrupt, "if you wanna talk to my fighter, speak with me first."

"Listen, pal, amateurs ain't allowed to have no managers."

"I'm his coach," I say, flatly.

He looks at my resolute expression and backs off. But he still hands Dino his business card. I yank it from Dino's hand, rip it up, and throw it on the floor. "Listen, pal, if you give my fighter another one of your shitty business cards, I'll bust your lip. I'm the coach."

He walks out pissed.

"You handled him good," chuckles Dom. "What did I tell ya? Boxing sucks. Sharks be cruising the water." He pats my back. "We trainers gotta stick together." Then he adds, "Give it some thought about you 'n me. I could use a smart college kid."

"Don't miss your callin', kid," whispers a voice from the past.

After everyone's gone, it's just Dino and me. I'm curious. "What's your plans?" I ask.

"Meeting Petey for a few drinks."

"No, I mean your plans for the future."

He chucks his wet towel into his dufflebag and looks at himself in the mirror.

These past six months have been a priceless morsel of life. But what's next? College? Job? Dino continues staring at himself in the mirror. Tonight's significance won't sink in till later. In time, Dino will understand what Dom Bufano had said: *Boxing enables a kid to transcend his shattered youth.*

Tonight, boxing led him to truth. And confidence. And health.

Boxing enabled him to see that he's worthy. Dino hacked away at his fear and cowardice. He murdered his hateful parts. He made *human cutlets* of himself. It'll take time to digest.

I love my heart because it is bitter, said Wallace Stevens.

Dino is still gazing at his face in the mirror. No bruises, cuts or black eyes. Now he's combing his thick black hair with a brush. Soon a new Dino will emerge. He'll start fresh. He'll begin to pick up the little pieces of his life, shard by shard, getting to understand each piece. And month-by-month, year-by-year, his life will improve.

"Nothing planned," he says, shadowboxing in the mirror. "Ref thought I was good."

Yeah, Dino, you could continue fighting and become ranked. Inter-city bouts…national bouts…international bouts…The

Olympics. You could follow in the footsteps of Sugar Ray Robinson, Emile Griffith, Mark Breland and Mike Tyson. Is that what you want?

"Boxing's crazy," I suddenly laugh. "Why do we do it?"

He stops punching and tilts his head back. It's like he's looking into his past…"Me and my Dad once met this old man sitting alone on the porch of a run-down hotel in Jersey…He was rocking back and forth in a wooden chair…His face was worn smooth like an old rock. 'See him?' whispered Dad. 'That's Joey Archer, the Uncrowned Middleweight Champion.' Dad said how Archer was once robbed in a title fight."

"Yeah, here, in The Garden, with Kid Gavilan."

"Dad asked him about Muhammad Ali's comeback with Larry Holmes. Archer said, 'You know why fighters come back, don'tcha?…We miss getting punched. We miss the closeness…We miss the human contact…'" Dino smiles a sad smile.

We hug.

That's when I kiss his forehead. "Take care of that kiss—it's from Jack Johnson." I explain the magical connection.

"Dino, any kid who can win The New York City Golden Gloves can do anything he sets his mind to. He only needs to believe in himself."

Praise—a potent force, a candle in the dark. It's love. It always works. It's magic.

Thanks, Dom. Thanks Jack Johnson.

On the corner of 33rd and 8th, a cool refreshing rain, like holy water, pelts my face. The night breeze licks my hair. I'm thinking about my mother…*My shutting you out for all these years was a conscious decision reached by an eight-year-old boy one night in the basement punching an Everlast heavybag with the purpose of hurting you*…Suddenly, I feel a small word scrambling on the wall of my skull. It's scuttling sideways, now it's backwards, now it's upside down…the word is *Forgiveness*…I nod.

Suddenly, someone taps my shoulder. Instinctively, I tuck my jaw and whirl around.

"Congratulations!" It's Tyrone Crooks.

"What're you doing here?" I say, composing myself.

"I be released yesterday. When I heard about you and Dino, I bought me a ticket."

I notice his short-cropped hair and clear eyes. He's lost the *fuck you* look. He appears older and more mature.

"I got my GED, Coach. And lined up a job," he smiles. "You get my letter? I be living close to the gym now."

I nod.

"Don't suppose our $25 bet's still on? I be in great shape, Coach. Doing 1,000 push ups a day. And I quit smoking, like you said."

"That's all good, Tyrone," I nod. "I see what you're after. Sure, boxing can purify you, but you need more than purification. You need someone to disinfect the walls of your skull. Or maybe an exorcism," I think to myself.

"Look, Coach, I ain't crazy no more. I was a low-life punk abusin' people. I know I be criminal with girls. I be horrible with everybody—you can tell me straight to my face. It's true. That's 'cause I be a weak little pussy. But I be readin' the Bible and I learn my lesson."

He clutches my arm, hard. "Coach, give me a second chance. Please. I wanna be somethin' more than I am."

"Why'd you key my car?" I ask, not that I cared anymore. I just wanted to hear it from him.

His eyes widen and he steps back. "I ain't gonna lie. I don't exactly know why. I honestly don't. But I apologize. I really do. And I'll pay for damages. Honest."

"How about the brick?"

"The brick?"

"You throw the brick?"

He looks down to the street in shame. He nods. "I'm sorry."

I look at Tyrone and sense a profound change. The arrogant smirk, the sniffling sense of superiority, the *fuck you, whitey*—gone.

"Please, Coach, train me."

For once, in Tyrone's eyes, I perceive honesty. But I know he's full of shit. He might have good intentions, but the streets will yank him back.

But every kid needs a second chance. Didn't I get one tonight?

I'm an English teacher. And coach. My job is teaching novels like *Catcher in the Rye* and plays like *The Miracle Worker*. But it's also to fight for kids and to offer them alternatives and devices to reclaim their lives.

"Stop by the gym, Monday," I sigh.

"Thanks, Coach, thanks," he says, grabbing my hand. "You won't be sorry. I promise."

Boxing is crazy stupid. But it's the one place where craziness and talent go hand in hand. Henry Miller, the author, said: *All human beings are insane until they discover their art.* Well, Tyrone's art might be boxing. Every stupid, crazy boy proved something important to himself tonight—he demonstrated discipline, honesty, guts and spirit. That's what made them winners. And artists.

Perhaps it's Tyrone's turn.

"Well," says Tyrone, "I gotta catch my ride back to White Plains."

"Train?"

"No, Ms. Tu."

My heart jumps. "Sing-Sing? Where?"

Beneath a street light, standing in the drizzle, clutching a fight program, is Sing-Sing. A golden halo envelops her, or maybe it's the streetlights. She's achingly beautiful.

Behind her is Tina.

"Congratulations," says Sing-Sing, walking closer. "Dino was magnificent."

"Yes, magnificent!" echoes Tina, flinging a punch in the air.

Tina seems different. Prettier. Her face is nearly healed and her hair is a natural auburn. Gone are the black, ripped fishnet stockings.

"Tonight was magic," smiles Sing-Sing.

I look into her eyes and grit my teeth. "Where the hell were you when I needed you?" I want to scream. But I'd be screaming at the wrong woman.

Sing-Sing touches my shoulder.

I want to punch her. And kiss her.

"I was wrong, Peter. You touch these boys."

I think of dogged Kirk and pathetic Herbie Pish. Stuttering Bobo. Fat Cockeye. Confused Black Earl. Crazy Tyrone. Criminal Street Mutt. Noble Tiger Green. Fragile Dino…Todd Rapier and my old stepfather…Somehow, I don't feel angry, inferior or frightened anymore.

"No," I say, reaching out to her, "they touched me."

This morning, about 7:00, I slip out of bed, careful not to awaken *The Little Terror of Mott Street.* She's sleeping on her side, softly breathing. The slant of the early morning sunlight catches the curve of her body. Her long black hair and delicate profile is a Monet pastel that I will draw, or adumbrate, one day. I wish that were true.

I wake up alone.

On the kitchen table is my resignation letter. I call Tyrone. His answering machine picks up.

I leave him Dom's gym number in Jersey City. Dom will train him. Tyrone will be Dom's next Golden Gloves Champ.

I put on soft music, and flip through the pages of my last journal. Kirk's sweat wafts up from the page; Dino's punches explode from my *flyspecks*…It's funny the tricks your mind plays on you. I had nearly lost 23 years to the lousy self image I carried of myself. I had ambushed myself into believing in my inferiority. I was so stupid to believe that the size of my boxing ability was the size of my weakness and fear.

I was so wrong to believe boxing was bad. Joyce Carol Oats says it best: *For all its shortcomings and danger, the ring is a perfect sanctuary, a precious counterworld, to the crazy world that exists outside of it. The ring is less verbally brutal, less economically unfair, and less politically abusive.*

I've rubbed souls with wonderful people in the ring.

Flipping through my journal, I can't stop thinking about Tyrone— his fly-catching speed and improved attitude. Why give Tyrone's championship to Dom?

I call Tyrone back.
This time he answers, breathing heavy.
"Running?"
"Three miles," he pants.
"Pinning your elbows?"
"Yeah."
"See you Monday. You're sparring Cockeye."
"Yes, sir."
My resignation letter lands in the trash.

EPILOGUE
WHERE ARE THEY NOW?

Tyrone Crooks: He became my next year's Golden Glove champion. He then went on to become an eastcoast champ, then an Olympic champ. He's currently on the brink of a world's title. I wish I could say that was all true. I wish I could say my boxing-enrichment program worked for him. I can't. After one month, Tyrone vanished.

Kirk Sloboda: He started a profitable landscaping business, sold it, and branched off into masonry. His company specializes in stonewalls, patios, sidewalks and cement foundations. During winter, it's commercial snowplowing. He hired Cockeye and pays him $80-$100 a day, off the books.

Scrawby Roach: After high school-and is currently in Iraq. He joined the Army.

Herbie Pish: He's married and drives a Fed Ex truck in Elmsford, New

York. Rumor is that his Honduran wife duped him into a wedding in order to obtain American citizenship. They have a baby boy—Chico.

Bobo Bowe: The gym's beta-dog worked as a nightshift tollbooth operator at the White Plains Airport. Then he started his own landscaping service. His business card reads:

> **"Let us look after you're garden style,**
> **quality work at compettive prices."**

Tiger Green: He continues training, hoping to jumpstart his pro career. One day while sparring Cockeye, his front tooth snapped. "I watch the fights on TV he laments and know I could beat those guys. If only I had the right management," No promoters have called.

Lola: She switched sports. She's a starting forward on the White Plains Girl's Varsity basketball team and averages 9 points a game. "Boxing's awesome! It's the only sport you can actually train side by side a pro athlete, like Tiger Green, and learn pro moves. In basketball you can't shoot hoops with Latrell Sprewell, or field grounders with Derek Jeter."

Street Mutt: After release from prison, he turned pro. His current record is 1-2. He was knocked out in his last fight. The knockout was so brutal, ESPN airs it weekly on its opening and closing credits. I still see him hanging out on the street corner smoking cigarettes.

Matt: **Matt Miller,** my pro-boxing student, metamorphosed into a famous raggae singer named Matisyahu. He is both on the leading edge of music culture and a member of an ultra Orthodox Jewish Community in Crown Heights, Brooklyn. After recovering from the visual shock of a Hasid rapping on MTV, you listen to his words and find insight and inspiration. Go, Matisyahu!

Dom Bufano: Dom died, so did his magic, little gym on the corner of Beacon Street and Oakland Avenue in Jersey City—God bles you Dom.

Dino Lazaro: He recently turned pro and is currently undefeated at 4-0. He's quickly emerging into a top middleweight prospect, and with a seasoned New York City trainer and a top promoter steering him, a world's title is a distinct possiblility. His next opponent? Himself,

Todd Rapier: He left teaching and is currently a principal of a Westchester public high school. He's finishing his doctorate and will pursue a superintendant's position in the future.

Sing-Sing: She gave birth to a beautiful baby girl, Zoe. She no longer teaches. She paints fulltime. She's my wife.

Carlos and **Black Earl:** I lost track of you two. Good luck to you both. And remember... *You know when a dream comes true? when you wake up.*

The End

APPENDIX
The Thirty Greatest NYC
Golden Gloves Champions

(Men)

Ratings are based upon number of titles won; quality of competition and accomplishments after The Gloves.

TOP TIER:

1. Sugar Ray Robinson
Two-time Golden Gloves Champ, 126 pound in 1939; 135 pound in 1940
World Welterweight and Middleweight Champion

2. Vince Shomo
The first four-time Golden Gloves Champ
Pan American Champion 1959

3. Emile Griffith
160 pound Golden Gloves Champ in 1957
Six-time World Champion

4. Mark Breland
The first five-time Golden Gloves Champ
Olympic Gold Winner 1984
WBA Welterweight Champion

5. Howard Davis
135 pound Golden Gloves Champ
Olympic Gold Winner in 1976

6. Alex Ramos
Four-time Golden Gloves Champ 1977-1980
National AAU Middleweight Champion 1979

7. Floyd Patterson
Two-time Golden Gloves Champ in 1951-1952
Olympic Gold Winner 1952
World Heavyweight Champion

8. Junior Jones
Two-time Golden Gloves Champ
World Bantamweight & Featherweight
Champion in 1993-94

9. The Spanakos Twins—Nick & Pete
NICK: Four-time Golden Gloves Champ at 118-126
pounds—1955; 1960-61; The 1960 Olympic Team
PETE: Four-time Golden Gloves Champ at 112-126
pounds--1955-56; 1960, 1964

10. Riddick Bowe
Heavyweight Champ Winner in 1984
Olympic Silver Winner 1987
World Heavyweight Champion

SECOND TIER:

1. Vito Antuofermo, World Champion

2. Michael Bentt (4 titles)

3. Hector Camacho (3 titles), World Champion

4. Gerry Cooney (2 titles)

5. Aaron Davis, World Champion

6. Mitch "Blood" Green (4 titles)

7. Zab Judah (3 titles), World Champion

8. Kevin Kelly (2 titles), World Champion

9. Juan Laporte, World Champion

10. Tami Mauriello

11. Wayne McGee (3 titles)

12. Buddy McGirt, World Champion

13. Dennis Milton (4 titles)

14. Eddie "Mustapha Muhammad" Gregory, World Champion

15. Davey Moore, World Champion

16. Jose Torres, World Champion

17. Davey Vasquez (3 titles)

18. David Villar (6 titles)

19. Coley Wallace

20. Chuck Wepner

The Five Greatest NYC Golden Gloves Champions

(Women)

1. Jill Emery

2. Veronica Simmons

3. Veronica Jeffries

4.) Kathy Collins

5.) Jill Mathews

Special thanks to: Bruce Silverglade, Bob Jackson, Bob Mladinich and Bobby Cassidy, Jr.